DATE DUE

MAR 16 '94			
MAR 16 '96			
DE 0 3 '12			

DEMCO

PLATE TECTONICS

Earth's Shifting Crust

PLATE TECTONICS
Earth's Shifting Crust

by SEAN M. GRADY

■ ■

The ENCYCLOPEDIA of
D·I·S·C·O·V·E·R·Y
and INVENTION

P.O. Box 289011 SAN DIEGO, CA 92198-0011

Library of Congress Cataloging-in-Publication Data

Grady, Sean M., 1965-
  Plate tectonics: earth's shifting crust / by Sean M. Grady

    p. cm.—(The Encyclopedia of discovery and invention)
  Includes bibliographical references and index.
  Summary: Discusses the history and development of
tectonic theory; how tectonics helps scientists predict
earthquakes and volcanic eruptions; and how engineers can
apply this knowledge to mining, cartography, and
designing buildings.
  ISBN 1-56006-217-7
  1. Plate tectonics—Juvenile literature.   (1. Plate tectonics.)
I. Title.   II. Series.
QE511.4.G73 1991
551.8—dc20   91-16714

Contents

■ ■

Foreword

The belief in progress has been one of the dominant forces in Western Civilization from the Scientific Revolution of the seventeenth century to the present. Embodied in the idea of progress is the conviction that each generation will be better off than the one that preceded it. Eventually, all peoples will benefit from and share in this better world. R.R. Palmer, in his *History of the Modern World*, calls this belief in progress "a kind of nonreligious faith that the conditions of human life" will continually improve as time goes on.

For over a thousand years prior to the seventeenth century, science had progressed little. Inquiry was largely discouraged, and experimentation, almost nonexistent. As a result, science became regressive and discovery was ignored. Benjamin Farrington, a historian of science, characterized it this way: "Science had failed to become a real force in the life of society. Instead there had arisen a conception of science as a cycle of liberal studies for a privileged minority. Science ceased to be a means of transforming the conditions of life." In short, had this intellectual climate continued, humanity's future would have been little more than a clone of its past.

Fortunately, these circumstances were not destined to last. By the seventeenth and eighteenth centuries, Western society was undergoing radical and favorable changes. And the changes that occurred gave rise to the notion that progress was a real force urging civilization forward. Surpluses of consumer goods were replacing substandard living conditions in most of Western Europe. Rigid class systems were giving way to social mobility. In nations like France and the United States, the lofty principles of democracy and popular sovereignty were being painted in broad, gilded strokes over the fading canvasses of monarchy and despotism.

But more significant than these social, economic, and political changes, the new age witnessed a rebirth of science. Centuries of scientific stagnation began crumbling before a spirit of scientific inquiry that spawned undreamed of technological advances. And it was the discoveries and inventions of scores of men and women that fueled these new technologies, dramatically increasing the ability of humankind to control nature—and, many believed, eventually to guide it.

It is a truism of science and technology that the results derived from observation and experimentation are not finalities. They are part of a process. Each discovery is but one piece in a continuum bridging past and present and heralding an extraordinary future. The heroic age of the Scientific Revolution was simply a start. It laid a foundation upon which succeeding generations of imaginative thinkers could build. It kindled the belief that progress is possible as long as there were gifted men and women who would respond to society's needs. When Antonie van Leeuwenhoek observed *Animalcules* (little animals) through his high-powered microscope in 1683, the discovery did not end there. Others followed who would call these "little animals" bacteria and, in time, recognize their role in the process of health and disease. Robert Koch, a German bacteriologist and winner of the Nobel Prize in Physiology and Medicine, was one of these men. Koch firmly established that bacteria are responsible for causing infectious diseases. He identified, among others, the causative organisms of anthrax and tuberculosis. Alexander Fleming, another Nobel Laureate, progressed still further in the quest to understand and control bacteria. In 1928, Fleming discovered penicillin, the antibiotic wonder drug. Penicillin, and the generations of antibiotics that succeeded it, have done more to prevent premature death than any other discovery in the history of humankind. And as civilization hastens toward the twenty-first century, most agree that the conquest of van Leeuwenhoek's "little animals" will continue.

The *Encyclopedia of Discovery and Invention* examines those discoveries and inventions that have had a sweeping impact on life and thought in the modern world. Each book explores the ideas that led to the invention or discovery, and, more importantly, how the world changed and continues to change because of it. The series also highlights the people behind the achievements—the unique men and women whose singular genius and rich imagination have altered the lives of everyone. Enhanced by photographs and clearly explained technical drawings, these books are comprehensive examinations of the building blocks of human progress.

PLATE TECTONICS

Earth's Shifting Crust

PLATE TECTONICS

Introduction

In the late 1960s, geologists came to a startling conclusion about how the earth's surface is shaped. Their findings astounded the world. They realized that the planet's outer crust is not solid but is made up of more than twenty separate pieces that slowly move over an inner layer of molten rock. These pieces, or plates, carry the continents across the earth as a conveyor belt carries boxes through a warehouse. The only difference is that the plates carry the continents around the curve of the earth rather than in a straight line.

As the plates collide with or grind into each other, they form mountain ranges, valleys, and even oceans. Plate movement also causes most of the natural disasters that occur throughout the world. The theory that accounts for plate movements in the past, the present, and the future is known as the theory of plate tectonics.

To develop the theory of plate tectonics, scientists had to reject the idea that the earth's surface was fixed and permanent. For thousands of years, people knew that erosion and natural disasters could cause land formations to change or disappear. People accepted that mountains and islands could vanish

▪▪▪ TIMELINE: PLATE TECTONICS

1 ❯ 2 ❯ 3 ❯ 4 ❯

1 ▪ 1650s
Archbishop James Ussher proclaims earth was created in 4004 B.C.

2 ▪ 1790s
James Hutton proposes "geologic time."

3 ▪ 1883
Eruption of Krakatoa.

4 ▪ 1906
Great San Francisco earthquake and fire.

5 ▪ 1908
Frank Taylor says all the continents originate from two gigantic landmasses centered over Earth's poles.

6 ▪ 1915
Alfred Wegener publishes his first book on continental drift.

7 ▪ 1935
Maurice Ewing makes his seismological survey of North America's continental shelf.

8 ▪ 1938 to 1945
World War II; first widespread use of sonar fathometers; submarine warfare spurs underwater research; Harold Hess discovers guyots.

9 ▪ 1952-53
Marie Tharp discovers a deep valley in the center of the Mid-Atlantic Ridge.

eventually, but no one believed that the continents could change their shape. The continents and their surrounding oceans were thought to be eternal, unchanging, and forever fixed in their positions.

Starting in the seventeenth century, however, geologists and other scientists began to question these commonly held "truths" about the world. Instead of relying on centuries-old theories, they made their own observations and drew their own conclusions about the way the land was made. They took long voyages to gather data and discussed their findings in universities and at conferences. And, as technology advanced, they replaced out-of-date discoveries with newer findings and ideas.

Drawing on these centuries of investigation, scientists were eventually able to take a look at the world and see its true structure. No longer was it necessary to depend on mystical powers or invisible forces to explain what created mountains or earthquakes. The theory of plate tectonics finally gave scientists and nonscientists alike an understanding of the forces that shape the earth. Gaining this knowledge, however, took years of persistence in the face of popular disapproval. And there are questions scientists still must answer before we have a complete picture of how the world works.

| 5 | 6 | 7 | 8 | 9 | 10 | 11 | 12 | 13 | 14 | 15 | 16 | 17 |

10 ■ 1959
Ewing, Tharp, and Bruce Heezen publish paper on Mid-Atlantic Ridge; subsequent data shows the ridge stretches around the world.

11 ■ 1960
Hess writes "History of Ocean Basins," suggesting the spread of the seafloor from the Mid-Ocean Ridge system as the force behind continental movement.

12 ■ 1963
Frederick Vine and Drummond Matthews claim bands of magnetized seafloor rock record ancient reversals in earth's magnetic field.

13 ■ 1965
Tuzo Wilson first suggests that earth's surface is made up of plates.

14 ■ 1968
Bryan Isacks, Jack Oliver, and Lynn Sykes show that earthquake records prove the existence of moving plates. They name this process "new global tectonics."

15 ■ 1975
Geologist Peter Coney identifies suspect terranes.

16 ■ 1980
Eruption of Mount Saint Helens in Washington state.

17 ■ 1989
Loma Prieta earthquake strikes near San Francisco.

From Giant Catfish to Continental Drift

Throughout history, humans have been victims of the violent effects of plate tectonics. Earthquakes and volcanoes have killed thousands of people and destroyed some of the earliest civilizations. In A.D. 79, the eruption of Mount Vesuvius in Italy destroyed the city of Pompeii, killing thousands of people. Similarly, the 1980 eruption of Mount Saint Helens in Washington state obliterated millions of acres of forest and spread ash over much of the nation.

Before scientists began to study why the ground shakes or why some mountains explode—in fact, before there were scientists at all—people believed that natural disasters were caused by spirits or gods. For example, an ancient Japanese legend blamed Japan's earthquakes on the *namazu*. The *namazu* was a giant catfish that lived underground and supposedly shook the earth to cause mischief. According to the legend, the creature's antics could be stopped only by the Kashima god, who would pin it down with a huge rock. The country's worst earthquakes struck when the god's attention drifted from the *namazu*.

Volcanoes, too, were explained by legends. To the Romans, they were forges of the blacksmith god, Vulcan. To Hawaiian Islanders, the volcano was the home of Pele, the fire goddess. These people and others blamed supernatural powers for making mountains explode.

Eventually, through observation, people began to find out more about the natural world. Much of their knowl-

In this rare painting, natives watch an 1840 eruption of Mount Saint Helens in Washington. Early natives gave supernatural explanations for volcanic activity.

The Greek philosopher Aristotle maintained that earthquakes were caused by a number of natural forces. His theories, though primitive, attempted to move beyond supernatural explanations.

edge came from the maps and tales of explorers. Other bits of knowledge came from people who looked for a more rational explanation of the world's behavior. Some early astronomers, for example, searched for a link between natural disasters and the way the stars, moon, and sun were arranged. Other scientists and philosophers felt that natural disasters were caused by a combination of forces. The Greek philosopher Aristotle, for instance, said earthquakes were the result of wind blowing through underground caverns. These winds built up pressure on the surrounding rock until the ground above shook to relieve itself of the strain.

Scholars also began to take notice of unusual features in the land around them. Travelers in southern Europe started noticing fossil seashells in the sides of mountains, far from the oceans. Scientists began questioning why the forces of erosion—wind, rain, rivers, and so on—had not long ago worn away the mountains. And with the discovery of the New World came perhaps the greatest puzzle of all: the shape of Africa's west coast seemed to fit, like a jigsaw puzzle, the shape of South America's east coast.

Attempts to explain the structure of earth began more than three hundred years ago. At that time, most Western civilizations thought that earth was only a few thousand years old. People believed that the Bible contained the true account of earth's creation. The Bible says God created the earth in a series of steps. First, he created land and seas and then made living creatures, including

Before the Age of Science, people relied on superstition and magic to explain the universe. Here, a medieval astrologer studies the location of the stars and planets.

man. Since most civilizations seemed no more than a few thousand years old, people figured the earth could not be much older.

They also believed that the planet's surface had always looked more or less the same throughout time. Any changes were made all at once during some violent event, probably the biblical Flood. This legendary disaster was a giant rainstorm that flooded the entire world. It was thought to be God's punishment for sins committed by humans early in earth's history. At one time, some Western scholars even thought that the Flood might have split South America apart from Africa. They said the tearing apart of the two continents would have created the matching coastlines. Most scientists and other scholars held similar views. Most importantly, people believed that earth was no more than six thousand years old.

This figure was determined by Archbishop James Ussher of Ireland who lived during the seventeenth century. Ussher wanted to settle the question of how old the earth was. He did this by adding up the life spans of the people mentioned in the Old Testament and counting back to the time of Creation. When he was finished, he proclaimed that earth's creation began the night before October 23, 4004 B.C. It ended, naturally, six days later.

The scholars of his day accepted his

For many years, people believed the age of the earth could be determined by studying the Bible. The biblical Flood was offered as an explanation for how the continents were shaped.

calculations partly because there was no way of proving them wrong. They had no means of measuring the age of rocks or fossils. Also, many people felt it was improper to contradict prominent scholars like Ussher. Ussher's calculations were considered the final word on earth's age for more than a century.

Hutton's Geologic Time

The idea of a young, essentially unchanging earth remained unchallenged until the late 1700s. Then, in Scotland, a geologist named James Hutton started thinking about mountains.

Hutton spent much of his time exploring the mountains surrounding the city of Edinburgh and other mountains in the British Isles. On these excursions,

James Hutton was one of the first geologists to question the idea that the earth was only six thousand years old.

Many theories about the age and formation of the earth were based on accounts from the Bible. In Genesis, God created the heavens and earth in six days.

he would examine rocks and note how they were positioned. One of his most important trips was along the North Sea coast of Scotland. He and a fellow scientist, John Playfair, found a cliff that piqued their curiosity. It was made up of two types of rock. The lower part of the cliff was a dark rock Hutton called "schistus." The upper part was made of horizontal layers of red sandstone.

The lower schistus layers had been tilted until they were nearly vertical. They looked like a row of books leaning to one side in a partially filled bookshelf. The two geologists knew that the schistus layers at one time must have been horizontal. The earth's gravity forces rock layers to lie flat as they

In this rock formation near Hancock, Maryland, different layers of sandstone and shale can be seen. By studying formations such as these, James Hutton and John Playfair determined that the earth was much older than most people thought.

form. The schistus could only have been tilted up after it had hardened. The tilting would have taken an immense amount of energy. But where would that energy have come from?

The geologists also noticed that the top of the tilted mass had been flattened by erosion before the sandstone formed because the boundary line between the rocks was level. Knowing that erosion on solid rock was extremely slow, Hutton and Playfair deduced that earth was far older than most people believed. Playfair later wrote about their discovery: "What clearer evidence could we have had of the different formation of these rocks, and of the long interval which separated their formation, had we actually seen them emerging from the bosom of the deep? . . . The mind seemed to grow giddy by looking so far into the abyss of time."

From these observations, Hutton developed the concept of "geologic time," the immense length of time it takes for landforms to develop and erode. He was one of the first to reject the idea that geology, the study of the earth's history and structure, must produce information that agreed with the Bible. Hutton's views were published as part of a biography Playfair wrote in the early 1800s. Naturally, Hutton's theory drew a great deal of criticism. Most scientists were taught and believed that the Bible's account of Creation was true. But a small group of scientists believed this biblical approach was incorrect. They, too, thought six thousand years was not long enough for the emergence of mountains and other landforms. And they applied Hutton's theories to their own investigations.

Cooling Earth Versus Rising Lands

Scientists still did not know how or why the earth's form changed over time. Geologists wanted to know what caused mountains to leap out of the earth. They wondered why volcanoes spewed out molten rock and why earthquakes kept shaking cities apart. Their main goal was to find the source of the vast amount of power needed to twist the earth's surface.

Scientists also had difficulty explaining many geologic oddities. They remained stumped by the presence of fossil shells in hillsides and why mountain ranges in North America seemed to echo the structure of European chains. A German explorer, Alexander von Humboldt, pointed out that rock layers under the soil of eastern South America were almost identical to those of western Africa, but he could not account for it.

In the mid-1800s, an American geologist found what he thought was the answer to these questions. James Dwight Dana had been trying to imagine a force powerful enough to create moun-

American geologist James Dwight Dana theorized that volcanoes were evidence that the earth's core was made of hot, liquid rock.

tains yet slow enough to work within Hutton's geologic time. Dana suggested that earth's volcanic activity was evidence that the planet was made of hot, liquid rock under a solid surface. And perhaps the entire planet had once been a ball of liquid rock that had slowly cooled and formed a skin.

Dana felt the key to the forces behind earth's activity was that as the planet cooled, the interior contracted and pulled the surface inward. The stress of the shrinking caused weak areas of the surface to fold into mountain ranges or sink into ocean basins. Dana compared this process to wrinkles forming on the skin of a drying apple. Earthquakes occurred as different zones of rock were fractured by the twisting crust. Volcanoes formed where molten lava could force its way up through broken rock.

This theory seemed to explain other puzzling scientific phenomena as well. Dana said fossil shells were left behind in the hills as water levels dropped to fill cavities in the crust. Similarly, identical formations on separate continents had once been joined by land bridges that long ago dropped below sea level as the planet cooled, Dana argued.

By the mid-1800s, Dana's view was accepted by the majority of the world's scientists. They felt it was the best explanation of why the earth's surface looked the way it did. Also, Dana was a well-known professor at Yale University, and the popularity of his theory was due as much to his respectability as to the theory's validity.

Even so, new studies of the earth soon challenged Dana's theory. One typical study was conducted by John Wesley Powell in the 1870s as he made a series of expeditions through the Grand Canyon. Powell was a veteran of the

The Colorado River's winding, circuitous course through the Grand Canyon (left) made John Wesley Powell (below) question whether the river was responsible for forming the Canyon. Powell made numerous journeys down the river and surmised that the land had been slowly pushed up, causing the river to cut down into it .

Civil War, a Union Army major who lost his right arm in battle. He lived for the thrill of adventure and the challenge of exploring unknown lands. After the war, he became interested in geology and geography. He decided he could best combine his interests by exploring the western frontier. And the Grand Canyon seemed to offer the most spectacular adventures of all.

On one of his journeys, Powell observed the path of the Colorado River through the Canyon. Powell knew that a river usually forms a canyon by carrying soil and rock from the side of a hill to the sea or to a larger river. The higher a river starts above sea level, the deeper the canyon it forms is.

But Powell noticed something odd about the Colorado River. Usually, rivers

that form canyons run a fairly straight and rapid course. The Colorado River, however, had cut a twisted, looping path through the Grand Canyon. At the same time, Powell realized that the canyon's hills and mesas could not have been present before the river came through. If they had been, the water would have taken a more direct path between them.

Powell and other scientists on his expeditions decided there was only one way the canyon could have formed. The Colorado River must have originally flowed over a flat plain from the Rocky Mountains to the Gulf of California. It wandered over the plain as it flowed. It even split into two or more streams, then joined back into one. Then, somehow, the land started rising and the river began cutting into the ground. Over millions of years, the river eroded the

land to produce the sides of the canyon. Powell's idea that the land had risen was not new. A British scientist, Sir George Airy, had a similar idea in 1855. He believed that mountains and the continents floated like icebergs over the lower layers of the earth's crust. The mountains and the upper layers of earth's crust are made up of granite, and the lower layers of a denser rock called basalt. This is why, Airy argued, mountains would float higher above the earth's crust—because they were made of a lighter material.

The idea that the continents floated like icebergs made some scientists wonder if they *moved* like icebergs as well. In 1908, American geologist Frank Taylor suggested that the continents were once two gigantic landmasses that "floated" over earth's poles at its top and bottom. Millions of years ago, he said, they

John Wesley Powell's camp on the Green River in Wyoming Territory. Powell's expeditions into the western wilderness made him question prevailing theories on how the earth was formed.

TAYLOR'S THEORY OF TWO ORIGINAL CONTINENTS

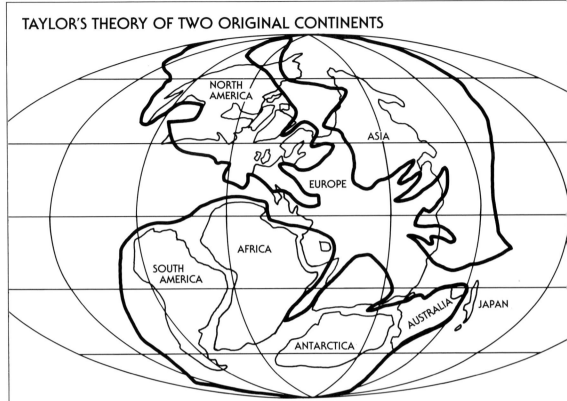

If placed side by side, the east coast of South America and the west coast of Africa fit together like the pieces of a jigsaw puzzle. In 1908 American geologist Frank Taylor used this fact to explain his theory that all seven continents once made up just two gigantic continents. One, containing what is now North America, Asia, and Europe, floated above the North Pole, and the other, composed of South America, Africa, Australia, and Antarctica, floated over the South Pole.

Then, millions of years ago, claimed Taylor, the two supercontinents started drifting away from the poles toward the equator. The drifting caused both continents to break apart, forming the seven continents we know today.

started drifting toward the equator. Like icebergs breaking apart in the ocean, the supercontinents pulled apart to become smaller landmasses. The southern landmass broke up into South America, Africa, and Australia. The northern mass split into Europe, Asia, and North America.

Why did the continents start drifting? Because of the moon, Taylor said. He believed that once, a comet had passed close enough to earth to be captured by the planet's gravity. This comet went into orbit around earth, becoming the moon. Taylor said that the supercontinents started moving in response to the moon's gravitational pull on earth.

Taylor was the not the first scientist to suggest the continents moved. This idea had appeared before, but it had usually been ignored. Most scientists thought that the idea of moving continents was too bizarre. Taylor's theory was treated the same way. But, as happens frequently in science, Taylor's basic idea later resurfaced when a German scientist noticed the same geographical features that had attracted Taylor's interest. The German, too, was struck by the fit of Africa and South America. This time, however, his ideas received more attention.

Alfred Wegener and Continental Drift

Alfred Wegener was a meteorologist, a scientist who studies weather. He was a well-known lecturer in his field at the University of Marburg in western Germany. But he also liked to read about developments in other scientific fields. So he often browsed through the university library. One day, he read a report about the discovery of identical plant and animal fossils in Africa and South America. The scientists who wrote the paper believed in James Dwight Dana's contracting-earth theory. Wegener knew about Dana's theories of folding continents and sunken land bridges. He may also have known of Taylor's drifting-continents theory, for he had a sudden vision of Africa and South America joined in a single landmass.

Wegener was not a geologist, but he did understand the basics of geology. After reading the report, Wegener began collecting information on other similarities among the continents. His research turned up a curious fact. Geologists had found evidence that a gigantic glacier had once covered much of the earth's southern hemisphere. They could tell

the glacier existed because it left deep scratches in the bedrock of South America, Africa, Australia, and India. Judging from the soil piled on top of the rock, the scientists calculated that the glacier existed about 280 million years ago.

Reading these reports, Wegener experienced a burst of disbelief. For the glacier to have covered India, it would have had to cross the equator. As an experienced meteorologist, Wegener knew this was impossible. No matter how cold the planet may once have been, the equator would have been too warm for the ice to stay frozen. Also, the scratches in the rocks showed the glacier had been moving under its own weight. But Wegener knew ice does not move like this over the open sea. He believed the glacier idea had to be wrong.

Wegener thought of a more realistic explanation of the glacier's formation. He grouped the countries that showed glacial remains around the South Pole. He connected them so that the areas affected by the ice sheet touched. When he was through, those areas matched each other almost perfectly. More significant, the shape of the reconstructed glacier closely matched the shape of present-day Antarctica.

Wegener took his reasoning a step further. He developed the idea that the world's continents had originally been part of a colossal landmass he called Pangaea, a name he created from the Greek words meaning "all land." About 300 million years ago, he said, this supercontinent began to break up. The pieces drifted off to become the continents of our own time. Though Wegener called this process "continental displacement," the theory became known as continental drift.

Wegener's views received worldwide

WEGENER'S THEORY OF CONTINENTAL DRIFT

FIGURE 1

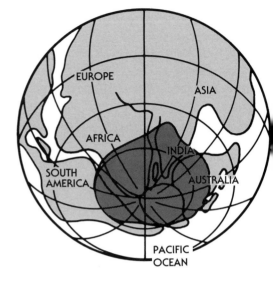

FIGURE 2

Paleontologists have discovered fossils and other geological deposits showing that regions of South America, Africa, India, and Australia (as indicated by the shaded areas in Figure 1) were all covered by the same glacier, or ice sheet, over 100 million years ago. Alfred Wegener, a German meteorologist, used this evidence to support his theory that all these regions were then located near the South Pole. In 1912, Wegener drew an unusual map showing South America, Africa, India, and Australia grouped together as a single continent around the South Pole. The coastlines of these landmasses all fit together perfectly. That led Wegener to theorize that they once formed the southern extreme of a single, gigantic continent (Figure 2) that began to break up and drift apart to form the continents we know today. He called this super-continent Pangaea.

attention after World War I, after they were published in English and French. His theories were controversial. Some scientists said that Wegener was unqualified to say how the earth's surface was formed because he was only a meteorologist. Others said that his theory did not explain how the continents started moving in the first place. This point was one that Wegener himself felt the the-

ory did not adequately address. Though he first suggested earth's rotation and gravity as the forces driving the continents apart, he later had to admit that the planet's crust was too heavy to be affected by them.

John W. Harrington, a professor of geology who began his career around this time, explains in his book *Dance of the Continents* why so many scientists ignored Wegener's continental drift theory: "We had all been taught the same dogma that continents and ocean basins were permanently fixed in their positions on the face of the earth. It took less effort . . . to accept this idea than to defend Wegener against the scorn of our colleagues."

But Wegener's work helped set the stage for the later discovery of plate tectonics. Despite its flaws, Wegener's theory presented a well-reasoned and well-documented case for moving conti-

nents. And not all the world's scientists rejected his idea. Some scholars felt that moving continents made more sense than the theory of a shrinking planet. Many in this smaller group were younger scientists who would still be alive when the theory of plate tectonics was developed. And Wegener's views also influenced the still younger generation of scientists who would piece together the clues that led to that discovery.

Cracks in the Earth

The proof that continents move came from a place that once seemed as unchanging as eternity itself—the bottom of the sea. For centuries, scientists thought of seafloors as wastelands. Marie Tharp, a twentieth-century geologist, said that until the late 1940s, seafloors were thought of as "saucers of great thicknesses of mud in a motionless abyss." Scientists knew that fish, whales, and other creatures live close to the surface of the sea. And many researchers thought of the deep bottom of the sea as a desert covered with water.

Twentieth-century geologist Marie Tharp recalls that early geologists thought of the ocean bottom as a motionless abyss.

During the early 1900s, scientists knew only a little about the seafloor. Explorers had measured how deep it was in some places. Scientists took samples of sea-bottom animals and rocks, using scoops attached to long ropes. They wanted to know more about what the seafloor looked like. But their equipment was too crude to do much more.

Explosions on the Seafloor

The discovery of plate tectonics began with the work of an American physics professor, Maurice "Doc" Ewing. Ewing was an expert in the field of explosion seismology, which means he used dynamite to create seismic waves, or shock waves in the ground like those of an earthquake. Each type of rock allows shock waves to travel at a different speed. Ewing recorded these waves on seismographs, machines that can measure even slight ground vibrations. By doing this, he could tell what types of rock the waves traveled through by timing how long they took to reach the machines.

In 1935, Ewing began to study the rocks that made up North America's continental shelf. Continental shelves are strips of underwater land that border a continent's coast. These shelves can extend for several miles before becoming cliffs that drop sharply into deep water. Some people thought shelves were an extension of the continent's

Through the technique of explosion seismology, American physics professor Maurice "Doc" Ewing was able to study North America's continental shelf.

granite bedrock. Others thought they were made up of sediments washed off the continent onto the basaltic ocean floor. Ewing believed that his explosion seismology techniques could settle the matter.

Ewing built a set of waterproof seismographs and lowered them to the shelf off the East Coast. He then set off a series of underwater explosions, creating shock waves that traveled through the water and into the shelf. Ewing knew that if the shelf were a single layer of granite, he would record two strong pulses. One pulse would come from the top of the shelf, and the other would come from the boundary between the shelf and the underlying basalt. If the shelf were made up of sediment, it would produce a number of smaller pulses. These returning shock waves would grow weaker as they were reflected by deeper and deeper layers. When he was done, Ewing pulled up

Maurice Ewing studies a map of the Atlantic Ocean on board his research ship Atlantis. *Ewing's work was instrumental in proving the plate tectonics theory.*

USING EXPLOSIVES TO ANALYZE THE OCEAN FLOOR

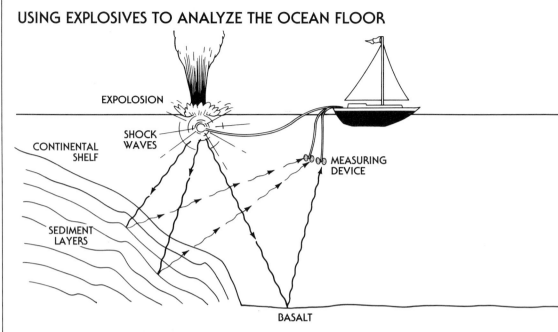

EXPOLOSION

SHOCK WAVES

CONTINENTAL SHELF

SEDIMENT LAYERS

MEASURING DEVICE

BASALT

Maurice Ewing was among the first to use explosion seismology to analyze the composition of the ocean floor and the continental shelves, which slope down from the edges of the continents to meet the ocean floor. He set off explosives underwater to create seismic waves, or shock waves. These waves traveled through the water to the ocean floor, or continental shelf, where they were measured by a waterproof seismograph.

Different surfaces under the ocean deflect seismic waves differently. For example, few waves penetrate hard, dense rock such as basalt. Almost all the waves are deflected. The seismograph would detect this as one strong pulse. If the waves hit loose sediment, however, most would penetrate right through it, and the seismograph would detect only a series of weak pulses. By analyzing the waves that bounce back to the seismograph, Ewing could determine the composition of the ocean floors and continental shelves.

the seismographs and analyzed their recordings.

The results surprised Ewing. They showed that the shelf was made of sediments piled on the basaltic ocean floor. But the covering was more than 2¼ miles thick. Ewing was amazed at the depth of the continental shelf. He also became curious about the rest of the world's oceans. Were all seafloors covered with sediment, he wondered. What was the seafloor like, say, in the middle of the Atlantic?

Ewing's work was important in proving several important points. He and later scientists were to gather information proving that ancient, sunken land bridges did not exist. The information they collected would also provide the clues that led them to discover the world's tectonic plates. First, however, Ewing had to overcome one setback. His study of the continental shelf had been paid for by a one-time grant from the Geological Society of America. Once the money was gone, Ewing had to return to his teaching job. At that time, not many people were interested in what the seafloor looked like. So Ewing's research was delayed. Finally, it was World War II that got Ewing actively studying the seafloor again.

World War II created a demand for information about the world's oceans. Submarine warfare devastated war fleets and merchant shipping in both the Pacific and Atlantic oceans. Submarines were so successful that the United States government felt that they would be used more and more in future wars. The government sought scientists who could make detailed maps of the seafloor so that submarines could safely travel farther and deeper. Also, submarine warfare had attracted popular attention to the world beneath the waves. Scientific organizations were eager to pay for

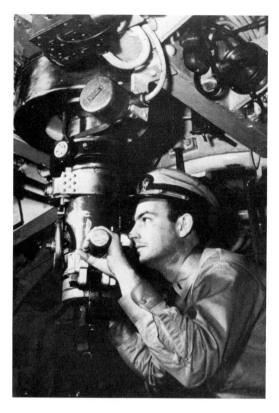

World War II brought about major discoveries that led to the theory of plate tectonics.

During World War II, the U.S. military needed accurate maps of the ocean bottom. Submarine warfare and voyages piqued an interest among military personnel and civilians about the world beneath the waves.

Geologists Marie Tharp (left) and Bruce Heezen were pioneers in mapping the ocean floor.

bring up samples of seafloor rock and sediment. He took equipment for gathering seawater at different depths. And he took along equipment for making as many other measurements as the expedition would allow.

The results of the trip were a complete surprise. The expedition members had expected to find the seafloor to be more than ten miles thick with mud layers billions of years old. But the explosion seismology experiments proved that very little sediment existed. The mud on the seafloor was no more than a few thousand feet—or 200 million years—thick. In some areas, they found layers of sediment from the past few thousand years right on top of layers millions of years old. For all they could tell, the planet had ceased to exist during the time between the two layers. What had happened to the "years" in between?

The most startling discovery was yet to come. Ewing lowered dredges when the expedition reached the slopes of the ridge. He expected to find at the very least a thin layer of recent sediment trapped beneath the ridge's peak. Instead, he found volcanic rocks, big lumps of lava much like those that are thrown out during volcanic eruptions. This type of rock is found only in land that formed in the recent geologic past—within the past few million years. The dredging also showed that the ridge had been created by an undersea volcano or something very much like one.

studies of the seafloor. Ewing, with his experience in underwater explosion seismology, received money from these sources to do more work.

In 1947, the National Geographic Society paid for a study of the Mid-Atlantic Ridge. The Mid-Atlantic Ridge is a north-south chain of underwater mountains in the middle of the Atlantic Ocean. It rises more than twelve thousand feet above the surrounding seafloor. The society hoped to find out why the ridge had formed exactly between the continents of Europe and Africa and those of North and South America.

The National Geographic Society asked Ewing to be in charge of the expedition. As he prepared for the trip, he decided to do more than just explosion seismology experiments. He took along dredges, large scoops that would

The Crack in the Earth

Two other trips to the ridge turned up similar evidence. In 1950, Ewing founded Columbia University's La-

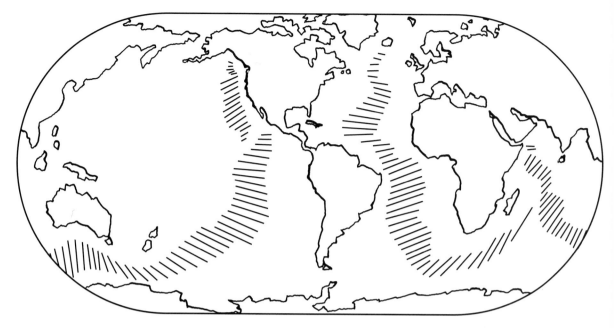

The discovery of the Mid-Ocean Ridge was instrumental in the formulation of the plate tectonic theory. A map shows how the ridge follows along the edges of the continents.

mont-Doherty Geological Observatory to serve as a center for his seafloor studies. Here, he and his colleagues were able to gather, arrange, and interpret data more easily than in their separate university offices.

During the voyages to the ridge, Ewing's team measured the distance between the surface of the sea and the top of the Mid-Atlantic Ridge. To do this, they used a device called a Fathometer. It measured the time it took for sound waves to travel through the water from Ewing's ship to the ridge and back. The faster the sound waves returned, the closer to the surface the ridge was.

Ewing asked a graduate student, Bruce Heezen, to make a map of the area using these Fathometer readings. Heezen, in turn, asked Marie Tharp, a fellow geologist at the observatory, to plot them on a map of the Atlantic. Tharp, like Heezen and Ewing, ex-

pected the map of the ridge to look like the map of a land-based mountain range. What she got was yet another surprise.

"As the . . . sketch emerged, Miss Tharp was startled to see that she had drawn a deep canyon down the center of the Mid-Atlantic Ridge," Heezen wrote about her discovery. At first, they did not really believe that the canyon existed. No one had ever heard of a canyon at the top of a mountain range before. And this canyon was spectacular. The range it ran through rose more than twelve thousand feet above the seafloor. Then, Heezen and other geologists showed that some of the world's major earthquakes had occurred along a line down the center of the canyon. This line went beyond the ridge and through the rest of the world's oceans.

This was the first major clue in the discovery of plate tectonics. Though none of the scientists knew it, the canyon marked the boundary of two tectonic plates. In the area Ewing studied, the North American Plate and the Eurasian Plate pull away from each other. The Mid-Atlantic Ridge marks the spot where molten rock seeps up between them. The stress of the spreading causes the earthquakes in that area.

As the 1950s progressed, more scientists began studying the ridge to find out how long it was, and other researchers found similar ridges in the rest of the world's oceans. Tharp and Heezen mapped the trail of earthquakes that extended south of the ridge. Combining their data, they discovered that the ridge followed the earthquake track on a forty-thousand-mile path around the globe.

The main line of this earthquake

British geophysicist Edward Bullard discovered that the ocean floor around the Mid-Atlantic Ridge was many times hotter than the rest of the Atlantic bottom.

route began north of Iceland and went down the center of the Atlantic. It rounded the southern tip of Africa, dipped south past Australia, and curved north through the Pacific Ocean. It went no closer to South America's east coast than two to three thousand miles away. It ended at the tip of Baja California, Mexico. Along the way, the earthquake route split into branches that went off in other directions. Part of it went into the Gulf of Aden along the southern edge of the Arabian Peninsula. And a small branch went west from the bottom of the ridge's Atlantic section almost to the southern tip of South America.

Tharp and Heezen's discovery of the huge ridge, called the Mid-Ocean Ridge, contradicted the prevailing notion that the earth was contracting. The Mid-Ocean Ridge could have been created only if the earth were expanding like an inflating balloon. But many scientists were unwilling to believe this new research.

Convincing the Skeptics

Fortunately, the work of a British geophysicist, Sir Edward Bullard, provided enough evidence to sway the skeptics. In the 1950s, Bullard took temperature readings along the mid-Atlantic portion of the ridge. He was investigating a theory that continents give off more heat than seafloors. According to the theory, continents are heated by deposits of heat-generating radioactive elements like uranium. Bullard expected the ridge to be very cold because it was in the middle of the ocean. But he found that the ridge was up to eight times hotter than the rest of the Atlantic bottom.

The only explanation for the excess heat was that the ridge was over an opening to the hot, molten mantle, a layer of the earth's interior that lies far beneath the crust.

Bullard's results showed that the earth could not be contracting. If it were, then a crack at the ridge would have closed almost as soon as it formed. His study also provided evidence that the crust of the earth was not a single mass. And an American geologist named Harold Hess soon used this evidence in an early description of plate tectonics.

Guyots and Geopoetry

Hess began collecting the information that would lead to his theory during World War II while he was captain of a U.S. Navy troop transport ship. His ship was equipped with a Fathometer like the one Ewing later used to survey the Mid-Atlantic Ridge. The machine was meant to be used during a beach assault in order to get the ship as close to shore as possible before landing the troops. Hess, however, saw it as a tool he could use to explore the seafloor. He decided to keep it running day and night while his ship was at sea.

As the Fathometer recorded the distance to the seafloor, Hess noticed some unusual underwater mountains. These mountains had flat tops, much like the mesas of New Mexico and Arizona, although they were hundreds of feet below sea level. Scientists had known of underwater mountains since the nineteenth century. But to Hess's knowledge, sea mountains this deep should have had definite peaks. They usually were not subjected to the wind and other forces of erosion needed to create

a flat top. Hess named these mountains guyots, in honor of a Princeton geologist from the 1800s. He identified more than twenty during his time at sea, but he could not explain how they had been created.

Hess assumed that the guyots had formed as volcanic islands where the seafloor was more shallow. Initially, they poked above the surface of the water and were subjected to the forces of erosion that gave them their "mesa" look. Then, somehow, they migrated off into deep water. But what caused them to move?

Hess was still puzzled by the guyots when in 1956 he heard of Marie Tharp's underwater rift. He had been talking with Ewing and Heezen at a geology conference when they mentioned her discovery. Hess became intrigued with the idea of this crack in the world. Could there be a connection between the rift with its volcanic activity and the formation of his guyots?

He went back to Princeton University and compared the data on these formations. Sure enough, he saw that lines of guyots seemed to stretch away from sections of the rift like seeds blown from a dandelion. He also noticed that the farther the guyots were from the rift, the deeper they were underwater. The younger, shallower guyots definitely formed on the younger seafloor Ewing had found near the ridges. But what could explain the presence of the older guyots in deeper water?

A Moving Seafloor

Hess was also intrigued by the lack of truly ancient seafloor sediment near the ridge. The continents had been eroding

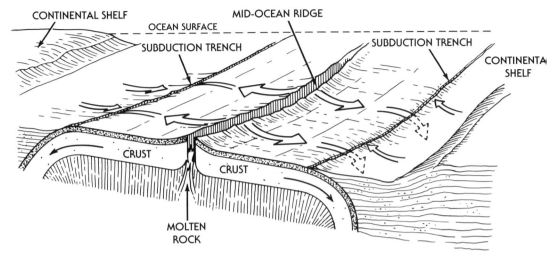

OCEAN RIDGES AND TRENCHES: RECYCLING THE EARTH'S CRUST

Mid-ocean ridges on the sea floor are really rifts, places where the earth's crust has pulled apart. From the mantle beneath the crust, molten rock pushes its way to the surface and flows out on both sides of a rift. As it cools and hardens, the molten rock forms ridges of new crust that push the old crust away from the rift in both directions.

In this way, the entire earth's crust is constantly moving in huge sheets, or plates, away from the rifts where they originated. As new crust is being formed, old crust is forced back down into the molten mantle. The plates that make up the crust on the ocean floor are made of heavy basaltic rock. When they collide with one another, the edge of one plate slips beneath the other and slowly descends back to the molten mantle. This is called subduction, and it creates a trench in the oceanic floor, called a subduction trench.

The plates beneath the continents are constantly colliding, too, but since the continental crust is lighter, these collisions do not cause subduction. Instead, the collision of continental plates causes the edges of the crust to bunch up into mountain ranges.

---

for billions of years, he thought. If so, why was there so little soil so far out in the ocean? Hess was also puzzled by a recent, curious discovery about the earth's crust. In the late 1940s, scientists had analyzed the crust under both the continents and under the oceans. They said the crust of the seafloor was only three miles or so thick. Continental crust, on the other hand, was as much as twenty-five miles thick. Why, Hess wondered, was the seafloor so thin?

As he thought more about the data, Hess wanted to know why the guyots should be the only part of the seafloor that moved. Could it be they had moved along with the surrounding seafloor?

This idea was an astounding intellectual leap for Hess. Up until then, he felt that ocean basins and continents were fixed objects. Saying the seafloor might move seemed as ridiculous as saying pigs might fly. But he could see that the guyots seemed to extend out from the Mid-Ocean Ridge. And if the seafloor itself moved, that might explain other curiosities. The mid-ocean seafloor would be too young for much sediment to have built up over it.

Hess saw that moving seafloors could cause the continents to move as well. He envisioned the continents riding the seafloor like automobiles on an assembly line. But unlike an assembly line, which is flat, the seafloor follows the curve of the earth.

In 1960, Hess wrote down his ideas in a paper called "History of Ocean Basins." In it, he suggested that the seafloors of the world's ocean basins spread out slowly from each side of the Mid-Ocean Ridge. Old seafloor was gradually reabsorbed by the planet's interior in deep trenches, places where the seafloor drops two to six miles beneath the surface of the ocean. Hess called this process subduction. The continents themselves are permanent features, he said. The spread of the seafloor simply tore them apart and pushed them back together.

Hess was very careful about sharing his views. He did not publish a paper on them until 1962, after first sending it to various friends and colleagues for review. He played down the radical suggestions he made and even introduced his paper as "an essay in geopoetry" rather than a serious, scholarly discussion.

This attitude worked both for and against him. The paper did not receive the angry criticism that surrounded Wegener's theory. Part of the reason may have been because Hess was writing as an insider, as a geologist. Also, the preceding decade's discovery of the Mid-Ocean Ridge may have left the world's scientists more receptive to new ideas.

Even so, many scientists and colleagues regarded Hess's work as a piece of science fiction. They agreed that shifting seafloors was an interesting idea, but they were not ready to overturn the century-old idea of fixed seafloors.

Hess's theory was not just a scientist's daydream. He had, in fact, described the mechanism of plate tectonics. And his ideas did excite a few, mostly younger scientists who were just entering the field. They began looking at the information from their work while considering Hess's data about seafloor spreading. At the end of the 1960s, they would show that Hess's theory had fallen just short of the truth.

Zebra Stripes on the Ocean Floor

Frederick Vine and Drummond Matthews were two of the younger scientists who thought Hess was right. They also believed that Wegener's theory of continental drift was correct. Their work provided concrete evidence that supported these two theories.

Vine and Matthews were geologists at Cambridge University in England. In 1962, they took part in a survey of the Indian Ocean that included magnetic measurements of the seafloor. As lava cools and hardens in the ocean, tiny pieces of iron oxide line up with the earth's magnetic field. Like little compasses, they point to the north magnetic pole and they stay in this position as the lava hardens. Scientists can measure the magnetic strength of these particles using a device called a magnetometer. During the survey, the ship towed a magnetometer over a portion of the Mid-Ocean Ridge. The device recorded a

A geologist uses a magnetometer. By using this device, Frederick Vine and Drummond Matthews theorized that the "zebra stripes" on the ocean floor were caused by the seafloor spreading.

stead of north. What could cause these miniature compasses to point away from the magnetic North Pole, he wondered. But he knew there was only one possible explanation. At some time, the planet's magnetic field had flipped upside down.

Further studies showed that the magnetic field had flipped over at least a dozen times. No scientists knew how this happened, and most considered it an interesting but useless geological oddity. In a flash of inspiration, however, Vine and Matthews saw this magnetic reversal as proof that the seafloor spreads.

If the seafloor formed as lava pushed its way up to the Mid-Ocean Ridge, it would contain tons of magnetic particles. These particles would be lined up with the earth's magnetic field as it was on the day they emerged. As the seafloor spread out from the ridge, the sections containing these particles would pull apart. This action would form bands of seafloor with magnetized iron oxide pointing in opposite directions.

Proving the Seafloor Moves

Vine and Matthews followed up on their burst of intuition by collecting more data to support their conclusion. They published a paper on their theory in the magazine *Nature* in 1963. This paper proved part of the theory that would be needed to prove that plate tectonics existed. It proved that the seafloor, and consequently the earth's crust, did move. But scientists still did not know that the earth's plates existed. And they were still skeptical of Vine and Matthews's ideas. The diagrams of the seafloor zebra stripes were pretty, but

horizontal pattern of strong and weak magnetic fields on either side of the ridge. Other scientists had recorded similar patterns near ridge segments in the Pacific Ocean. They called them "zebra stripes." No one knew what caused them.

When the voyage was over, Vine and Matthews tried to find an explanation. They discussed how the zebra stripes might relate to Hess and Wegener's theories. They also tried to discover a connection between the stripes and the reversals in the earth's magnetic field. Since 1906, scientists have known the magnetic field is not stable because of the work of Bernard Brunhes. A French physicist, Brunhes studied volcanic rocks that formed on land millions of years ago. In them, he discovered particles of iron oxide that pointed south in-

SEISMOGRAPHS AND SEISMOMETERS

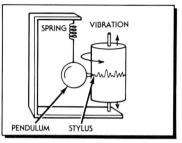

VERTICAL MOVEMENT

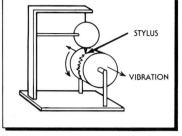

HORIZONTAL MOVEMENT

SEISMOGRAPH

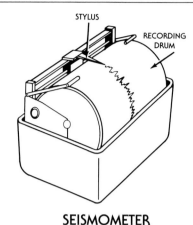

SEISMOMETER

In a seismograph, a pendulum, supported by springs, is suspended so that it remains perfectly still. Attached to the end of the pendulum is a stylus, or pen, that touches a sheet of paper on a recording drum. The paper rolls exactly the same distance every hour.

Any movement of the earth will cause the drum to vibrate, while the pendulum remains still. As a result, the pendulum will trace the exact vibration on the paper. To be accurate, a seismograph must contain three pendulums: a vertical one to trace vertical vibrations, and two horizontal pendulums to trace horizontal vibrations in all four directions.

Today, most seismologists use seismometers. A seismometer is an electronic seismograph. Inside the seismometer are three pendulums, each containing a fine electric coil. Each pendulum is suspended between the two opposite poles of a magnet. Any vibration of the magnet causes an electric current to pass through the coil. The stronger the vibration, the stronger the current in the coil. This current is relayed to a stylus, which marks the vibration on a paper drum.

scientists demanded recent proof that the seafloor moves.

The person who supplied the proof was Tuzo Wilson, a geophysicist at the University of Toronto. Wilson had been impressed with Vine and Matthews's discovery. He was so impressed that he started working with Vine to improve upon the paper's findings. Together, they collected more magnetic data on the spread of the seafloor. And as the data came in, Wilson was able to apply it to one of the last great puzzles of the Mid-Ocean Ridge.

The Mid-Ocean Ridge looks like a ruined stone wall. It is broken into segments that are slightly to the left or the right of each other. These segments are separated along small fractures that gradually vanish as they lead out from the ridge. Previously, scientists using seismographs had found that many earthquakes occur along these fractures. Until the mid-1960s, scientists had assumed these fractures were similar to normal land-based earthquake faults.

Wilson compared the seismic records with the new magnetic surveys of the ridge. The zebra-stripe magnetic patterns acted as signposts showing which way different sections of seafloor spread. He saw that earthquakes occurred only where sections of seafloor moved in opposite directions. As soon as these segments passed each other, the earthquakes stopped. Wilson knew this was not how an earthquake fracture, or fault, usually behaved. On land, earthquakes occur all along a fault, not just in some areas. Something different must be happening along the ridge, Wilson thought. But what was it?

Wilson came up with a simple explanation. He theorized that the earth's surface had ripped open unevenly, fracturing the crust as it pulled apart. The uneven parts of the ridge were created at this time. He theorized that earthquakes happened only in areas between the uneven segments. The seafloor sections would then have moved in opposite directions in these areas. Once past the uneven ridge parts, the seafloor would spread in one direction. Wilson called these underwater faults "transform faults." The name came from the way the seafloor switched from one type of action to another.

The theory still needed a bit more work before Wilson was satisfied with it. He had based the existence of transform faults on Hess's idea that seafloors spread. But Hess had not said how seafloor spreading related to the earth's surface as a whole. Wilson said that the Mid-Ocean Ridge and its transform faults were part of a world-wide network of geological formations. This network included deep ocean trenches marked by arc-shaped chains of volcanic islands. Combined, these formations separated the earth's surface into a number of smaller blocks that moved freely over the mantle.

Wilson did not describe the movement of these blocks. He did not even give their existence a name. Nevertheless, his was the first description of plate tectonics. And his description marked the start of a geological revolution.

The Jigsaw Puzzle Completed

In his book *Dance of the Continents*, geology professor John Harrington says the development of the plate tectonics theory was like the solution of a jigsaw puzzle. "All of a sudden, there was order; everything had its place. Even the blank areas had well-defined shapes that indicated what to look for next." As the decade progressed, scientists refined and expanded on Wilson's ideas.

The first scientists to follow up on Wilson's "blocks of crust" idea were Dan McKenzie and Robert Parker, two British geophysicists. They had been studying records of the world's earthquake zones—areas where earthquakes are most likely to happen. For centuries, scientists did not know why some areas were more likely to form earthquake faults than others. It seemed that nature created earthquakes merely on a whim.

McKenzie and Parker knew better than that. They made a chart of the world's earthquakes. They saw that most earthquakes occurred in fairly narrow belts over the earth's surface. Their pattern was similar to, and in many places overlapped, Wilson's network of ridges, trenches, and volcanic islands. This, they figured, was no coincidence. There had to be a connection. So in 1967, they published a paper saying the world's earthquake zones supported the idea that giant "paving stones" make up

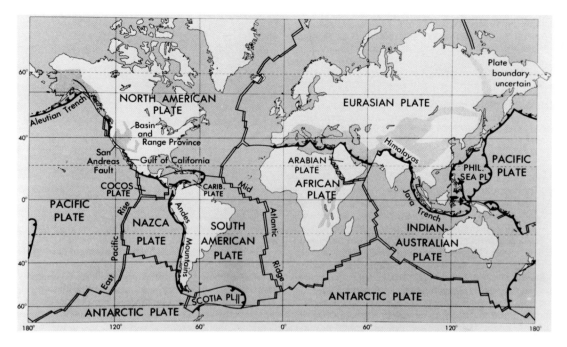

A simplified map of the plates of the world. Areas marked with double lines are the spreading zones. The lines with a barb show subduction trenches. Areas marked with a single line show strike-slip faults. Stippled areas show active faults.

the earth's surface.

A more detailed study of earthquakes in 1968 produced another significant discovery. Bryan Isacks, Jack Oliver, and Lynn Sykes were seismologists at the Lamont-Doherty Observatory. They examined what types of earthquakes occurred along the supposed plate boundaries. If the plates originated along the Mid-Ocean Ridge, then earthquakes in that area would gather near the surface, they thought. The top of the ridge would shatter as new magma—molten rock inside the earth—worked its way up from the mantle. And earthquakes along the transform faults would not start deep in the earth's crust. They were not surprised when their investigations showed their idea was correct.

Likewise, they expected to find quakes deep in the earth along the ocean trenches. Hess had suggested these areas were where old seafloor returns to the mantle. The Lamont scientists figured the seafloor of one plate would have to travel far under the other before it started to melt. If so, there should be powerful earthquakes far below the bottom of the sea. Fortunately, the proof for this already existed. A geophysicist named Hugo Benioff had plotted ocean trench earthquakes in the 1940s and 1950s. His studies agreed with the Lamont scientists' theory. The three scientists named the theory "new global tectonics." *Tectonics* comes from the Greek word *tekton*, which means "builder." Eventually, the theory became known as simply "plate tectonics."

Naming the theory did not mark an end to the process of discovery about the movements of the earth's crust. Scientists still do not know why the plates move as they do. And there have been many other discoveries that have enhanced what scientists already know. Even so, the discovery of plate tectonics forced people to change the way they looked at the earth. The planet's surface was no longer a solid, mostly unchanging structure. Instead, it was fluid. And it never stops changing, although the transformations are too slow for people to see.

For scientists, the discovery led to a surge of understanding about why the planet's surface looks and behaves as it does. Seismologists—scientists who study earthquakes—were finally able to point to the cause of earthshaking tremors. Volcanoes, once thought to be the homes of gods, were now seen as holes opened in the shifting earth. And people everywhere had a theory that would eventually be used to seek out new sources of energy and raw materials.

CHAPTER 3

Tracking and Predicting Earthquakes

Earthquakes are the most obvious side effect of the movement of the earth's plates. Most of the earthquakes that affect human beings occur along the edges of the plates. The three Lamont-Doherty Observatory scientists even used earthquakes to prove the existence of plate tectonics. At the same time, they described how the movement of the earth's plates caused these natural disasters. Their work led other scientists to concentrate their earthquake studies on the areas where quakes are born.

An Early Idea About Earthquakes

The earth's plates move far too slowly for most people to tell they move at all. Most plates take five years or more to move a single foot. Many people find it hard to understand how the plates can cause the fast, violent shaking that comes with a major quake. It seems that the plates' movement is slow enough for the land or the seafloor to adjust to its new shape.

In the early 1900s, a scientist named Harry Reid began to study how the earth responds to plate movement. Reid was a seismologist, and he had been in charge of an investigation of the San Francisco earthquake of 1906. During this disaster, a very powerful earthquake shook the ground underneath the city. Many buildings were shaken apart. Chimneys toppled into the broken streets. Buried cable car lines were twisted out of shape. Worst of all, the city's water pipes were twisted and pulled apart. Soon after the earthquake,

Seismologist Harry Reid (pictured here with his research team) studied the effects of the 1906 San Francisco earthquake on the earth's surface.

The San Francisco earthquake of 1906 rumpled roads, tore buildings, streets, and trolley tracks in two, and toppled buildings.

fires broke out and began spreading. Without any water, the fire department could not keep the blaze from destroying most of the city.

Naturally, Reid had no knowledge of plate tectonics. At this time, Alfred Wegener had not yet come up with his theory of continental drift. In 1885, however, a geologist named Andrew Lawson had found a fault underneath San Francisco. It was as if someone had taken a thin knife and sliced into the earth, leaving a tiny gap. Reid wondered if this fault had caused the great quake. And if so, was that earthquake the only example of land shifting along this line?

To answer these questions, Reid studied land survey reports made as much as fifty years before the 1906 earthquake. His studies revealed a curi-

At the time of the 1906 quake, scientists knew nothing about the movement of the earth or its plates. They were puzzled by some of the effects of the quake. Here, the earth on either side of the fence has moved in opposite directions, splitting and moving the fence apart.

ous fact about the land on both sides of the fault. Every stream that crossed the fault near San Francisco curved to the north. Roads and fences built across the fault had also been bent northward. Reid found the answer to his second question. The area *had* been moving long before the earthquake.

Reid soon had the answer to his first question as well. Teams of scientists had gone into the country around San Francisco to investigate other quake damage. Their findings were as amazing as the reports Reid had just read. The streams, roads, and fences along the fault had been split in two. Roads heading east from the ocean would break at the fault and shift to the right. Across the fault, a road would start again as much as twenty feet to the south of its original path. Reid said this phenomenon proved the quake had been caused by land slipping along the fault line.

Actually, Reid said that the land had not so much slipped as snapped for-ward. Rocks are elastic, he said. With enough pressure, they can be made to bend a little. Somehow, miles-long blocks of rock on each side of the fault started to bend out of shape. The contact between the edges of the rock kept these blocks from sliding past each other. Eventually, the strain of the bending became too intense. The rock on each side of the fault let go and snapped forward, one side heading north and the other going south. After the snapping, Reid said, each block returned to its original shape.

Plate Tectonics and Earthquake Mechanics

Reid, of course, was not talking about blocks of the earth's crust as we know them today. Instead, he was talking about blocks of land only a few hundred miles long on any side. These blocks, he thought, were created as various pressures cracked apart the bedrock of North America. He probably also believed that these blocks were bent by contractions of the earth's surface. Although he was wrong about these points, the plate tectonics theory shows that Reid's ideas were very close to the truth.

Lynn Sykes, Jack Oliver, and Bryan Isacks undoubtedly knew of Reid's earthquake model. Their work, however, showed that Reid had described only part of the earthquake process. Earthquakes do occur when blocks of rock snap forward. The slipping, they said, is just part of the process, however.

Some tectonic plates grind next to each other as they move over the mantle. Like two erasers rubbing against each other, the plates grab onto and snap away from each other. This tectonic "skittering" is what Reid described in his description of earthquake movement. The San Andreas Fault in California marks one of these tectonic boundaries. The fault lies along the border between the North American Plate and the Pacific Plate.

The world's most violent earthquakes occur at the earth's subduction zones, areas where one plate dives beneath another. The diving plate bends down sharply as it slides beneath the earth's crust toward the mantle. There, it slowly melts and is eventually recycled as volcanic lava or new seafloor.

The combination of sliding and bending creates tremendous pressure

A three-dimensional drawing of the San Andreas Fault in California shows where the Pacific Plate and the North American Plate split the state into three parts. Movement along these plates is what causes the many earthquakes that plague California.

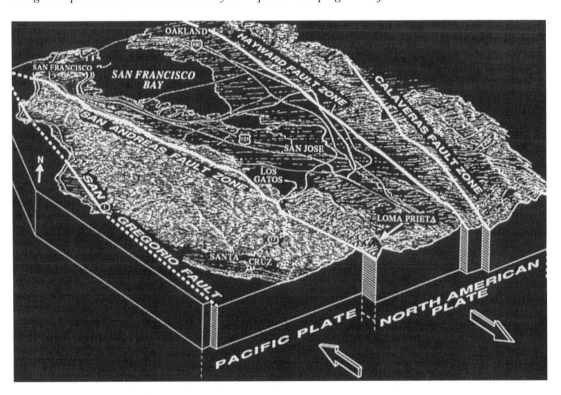

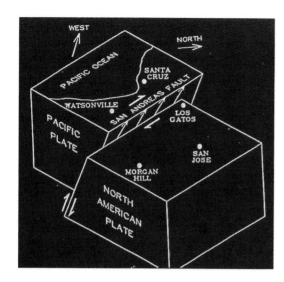

This schematic drawing depicts movement along the Pacific Plate and the North American Plate along the San Andreas Fault.

released in just a few minutes.

Japan has been a victim of the violence of these earthquakes. The islands of Japan sit just above one of the deepest ocean trenches in the world. Every year, Japan is shaken by more than one thousand large and small quakes. Occasionally, these quakes have been large enough to destroy cities. One of Japan's worst earthquakes took place on September 1, 1923. More than 140,000 people were killed, and hundreds of thousands of buildings were destroyed in Tokyo and Yokohama. Much of the damage was caused by giant firestorms created by ruptured gas lines and by rapidly burning wood and paper buildings.

Some other land-based earthquakes are caused by continental plates colliding with each other. Colliding continents do not form subduction zones as colliding seafloors do. Continents are made up mostly of granite, which is too light to sink into the magma beneath it. Instead, the continents slowly push against each other, and their edges

on the rock. Often, the top of the diving plate will become jammed against the bottom of the other plate. As the diving plate pushes forward, it will build up pressure against the top plate. Suddenly, the rock of the diving plate will leap forward and down. All the pressure will be

The earth's most violent earthquakes occur at subduction zones, where one plate dives under another. Japan is affected by these types of quakes. A quake centered in Tokyo in 1923 killed more than 140,000 people and ruptured gas lines, which led to huge firestorms.

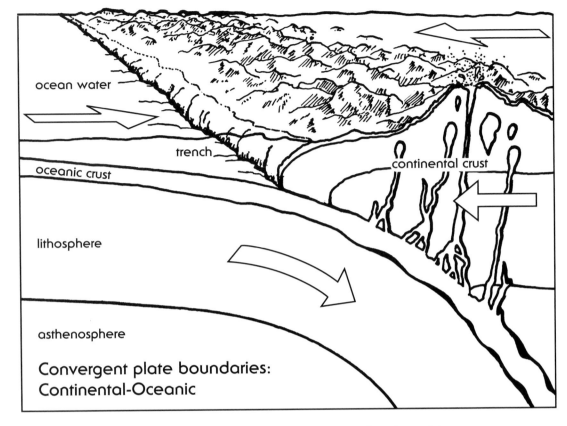

ocean water

trench

oceanic crust

lithosphere

asthenosphere

continental crust

**Convergent plate boundaries:
Continental-Oceanic**

A schematic drawing depicts the effects of plate tectonics. Here, moving plates of the lithosphere are driven together by currents in the asthenosphere. Mountains form as the plates are pushed forward.

bunch up into high mountain ranges. At the same time, weak areas along the border of the two continents break and slide past each other under the pressure of the collision. The same thing happens in zones of weaker rock hundreds of miles away from either side of the border.

The most dramatic example of the result of this process is the Himalaya Mountains. These are the world's highest mountains. For centuries, people living near them have called them "the roof of the world." They were created as India rode north on the Indo-Australian Plate and collided with Asia. For millions of years, the land of India has

been shoved against this larger continent. Eventually, India will be transformed into one large mountain range on the southern coast of Asia.

Predicting Earthquakes

For most of the twentieth century, seismologists have been searching for a way to warn people of coming earthquakes. Their hope has been to give people at least a few minutes to get to shelter. But the problem in reaching this goal is that no one really knows how the earth is going to behave.

There have been a few successes in

The Himalaya Mountains, the largest mountains of the world, were formed by plate activity. These mountains were created millions of years ago, when the Indo-Australian Plate collided with Asia.

predicting earthquakes. One of the best examples was a prediction made before the October 17, 1989, earthquake at Loma Prieta near San Francisco, which interrupted a game of the World Series. More than a year before that earthquake, a group of scientists published a report on the San Andreas Fault. They had just finished analyzing new data about past earthquakes along the fault. Their goal had been to see what areas stood the greatest risk of experiencing a large-scale earthquake in the near future. The results showed that the segment where the Loma Prieta earthquake occurred had the best chance for such a quake.

The prediction did not name a specific day for the quake. The actual prediction was that the Loma Prieta segment stood a 30 percent chance of having the quake within thirty years. This is like saying a person stands a one-in-three chance of wrecking his or her car before he or she turns fifty. In a sense, it was a matter of luck that the quake hit so soon after the scientists' prediction.

As Scottish geologist James Hutton pointed out, the earth works according to slow, steady geologic time. For scientists to be able to pin down an earthquake to even a thirty-year time frame is a big achievement.

That scientists have been able to make any predictions at all is due to research into the effects of plate tectonics. The plate tectonic theory gave scientists an overall view of what causes earthquakes. But this knowledge did not give them the details they needed to say when a section of a plate was going to snap forward. It did not tell them how much strain a fault line could handle. Fortunately, it did show them where they should look to find this information.

The evidence that earthquakes gather along tectonic boundaries refocused seismological research. Earlier in the twentieth century, some seismologists believed earthquakes came from areas of a fault where more pressure on the rock had built up. They thought that small earthquakes acted as safety valves to relieve this tension. And they

This collapsed freeway was caused by an earthquake. Because scientists have not been able to predict when an earthquake may occur, many people are injured on roadways or in collapsing buildings.

thought that patterns of earlier quakes could be used to predict when and where new quakes would strike.

This idea seemed to fit in with the plate tectonic theory. The skittering of the plates would account for areas of tense and relaxed rock. Further research into plate movement showed each plate moves at a fairly constant speed, measured in inches per year. Seismologists felt that this constant movement should cause regular earthquakes along the plate boundaries. A segment of the boundary that had not had any recent tremors, they reasoned, was more likely to be the site of a major earthquake. These segments became known as seismic gaps.

The seismic gap theory still needed to be proven before scientists were willing to accept it. Then in 1971, Lynn Sykes noticed a number of seismic gaps along the southern coast of Alaska. This area was where the northern edge of

the Pacific Plate dives under the North American Plate. Sykes said these areas would probably be hit by earthquakes within a few decades. A year later, a large earthquake struck one of these gaps, near the town of Sitka. The seismic gap theory seemed to have been proved. But would monitoring these gaps help scientists say exactly when an earthquake was coming?

A scientist from the California Institute of Technology named Karen McNally answered this question in 1978. McNally was visiting Mexico City when a seismic gap near Oaxaca, a city on the southern coast of Mexico, came alive. Mexico's south coast lies over a subduction zone. A very small tectonic block called the Cocos Plate moves northeast from a segment of the Mid-Ocean Ridge. This small plate dives under Mexico, which lies on the North American Plate. The Institute of Geology in Mexico City recorded small earthquakes within a few weeks of each other. McNally wondered if these quakes might be setting the stage for a major earthquake. If they were, this would be a perfect chance to get some much-needed earthquake data.

Using Seismometers to Predict Future Quakes

McNally convinced the institute's geologists to set up a string of seismometers along the gap. As they collected more data on the small quakes, they noticed an unusual pattern. The earthquake waves were moving from one edge of the gap toward the center. It was as if the center of the gap were locked more tightly against the edge of the subduction zone than its edges. McNally figured the gap was getting ready to leap forward.

That is exactly what happened. On November 28, a large earthquake hit Mexico "right in the middle of our [seismometer] array," McNally later said. No-body was hurt during the earthquake, because few people lived near where the quake was strongest. People in Mexico City, about three hundred miles from the quake, felt only a few tremors. Yet the seismometers along the gap gave McNally records of all the earth movements leading up to the big quake. She had proven that monitoring seismic gaps along plate boundaries can help predict future quakes.

This success spurred other scientists to closely monitor seismic gaps. One of the most intensive of these studies is taking place near Parkfield, California. Since 1985, the U.S. Geologic Survey (USGS), along with the California state government and universities, has studied a sixteen-mile segment of the San Andreas Fault. They have buried machines that measure the amount of strain being put upon the rock in the area. They have set up lasers to measure how fast land slips along the fault. And they have installed hundreds of seismometers to measure small earthquakes generated as the earth shifts.

Strain meters measure the amount of strain being put upon rock by plate movement. Here, a researcher records the strain meter's findings.

The USGS chose the Parkfield segment of the fault because it has a history of regular earthquakes. Since 1857, moderate earthquakes have been reported along the segment about once every twenty-one years. The last major earthquake in the area took place in 1966. Therefore, scientists think a major quake will hit the area by 1993.

Other scientists are not so sure this method works. Tousson R. Toppozada of the California Division of Mines led a group that studied the history of Parkfield's earthquakes. He did not think that any area of a fault could follow such an exact earthquake timetable. So the group looked over old newspaper articles and letters that mentioned earthquakes near Parkfield. They turned up two earthquakes that did not fit in with the twenty-one-year cycle. They also found evidence of smaller earthquakes that followed two of the area's "regular" earthquakes.

When Toppozada's group put all this information together, they came up with a startling conclusion. The Parkfield segment has had only two large earthquakes since 1930—one in 1934 and one in 1966. Before 1930, it had had seven—one each in 1857, 1877, 1881, 1901, and 1908, and two in 1922. According to the apparent pattern, the 1922 quake should have been followed by a quake around 1944. Seismologists thought the 1934 earthquake was a one-time event that kept the 1944 quake from happening. But Toppozada's group said the pattern was only an illusion. According to their data, the Parkfield segment was calming down.

Even so, the scientists studying the Parkfield segment still feel it is due for a large earthquake. If the earthquake finally does hit, Parkfield will be one of the best-observed quake areas in the world. Scientists hope to use the knowledge they gain to give more accurate earthquake warnings.

Deadly Waves

Accurate predictions would give people time to prepare for earthquakes. Even a few minutes' warning could give people enough time to get to a safe area in their homes or offices. Accurate earthquake predictions would also help save lives in coastal cities. People living next to the ocean have to watch out for giant sea waves called tsunamis.

These waves are created by the sudden collapse of land underwater. Sometimes, underwater earthquakes trigger huge landslides near a continent's coastline, pushing water out of its way. At other times, stretches of seafloor along a subduction trench leap forward and down. Millions of tons of seawater rush in to fill the space the land leaves behind. The force of the rushing water heads on toward the coast as a huge wave. The water is so powerful that it can also rebound off the seafloor and the nearby coastline to create a pulse in the water strong enough to travel across oceans.

The pulse cannot do any damage to ships in the middle of the ocean. At sea, its force is spread out between the surface of the water and the ocean bottom far below. It can lift the ocean surface only a couple of feet. The damage comes when the pulse reaches an island or a coastline.

As the seafloor rises, the pulse becomes more powerful. The wave it creates becomes steadily larger. Soon the wave can be as high as one hundred

COMPARING THE POWER OF EARTHQUAKES USING THE RICHTER SCALE

1.0

2.0   (10 X 1.0)

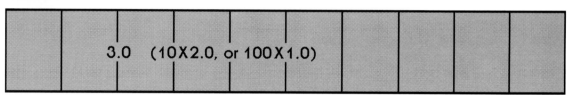

3.0   (10 X 2.0, or 100 X 1.0)

Seismologists rate the strength of the world's earthquakes according to the Richter scale. This guide to earthquake intensity was invented around 1935 by Charles F. Richter.

Before Richter invented his scale, scientists ranked earthquakes based on how much damage the quakes caused. The scientists looked at land and buildings that had been through an earthquake. They found out what people felt during the quake. The scientists then compared this information to a scale that listed twelve levels of earthquake damage. The more damage the quake caused, the stronger it was thought to be. This scale had been developed in 1902 by Italian seismologist Giuseppe Mercalli. Other seismologists modified it during the next few decades.

Richter was a scientist at the California Institute of Technology's Seismological Laboratory. He was not happy with this method of measuring earthquakes. Richter had been comparing seismometer recordings of earthquakes with on-scene reports from scientists. He realized that a very strong earthquake in a remote, uninhabited area could receive a low rating. Likewise, a small earthquake in the heart of a city could be rated higher than it deserved. So Richter created his own scale. He based his scale on an earthquake's actual strength as recorded by seismometers rather than on the damage it caused. Richter called this strength the earthquake's magnitude.

The Richter scale is the worldwide standard for earthquake measurement. Zero magnitude on the scale is equivalent to the shaking caused by blowing up a pound of dynamite. An earthquake with a magnitude of 1 is ten times stronger than that exploded pound of dynamite. Most people cannot feel earthquakes with a magnitude lower than 3. The 1989 Loma Prieta earthquake measured 7.1 on the Richter scale.

feet or more. It can carry water far inland. As it travels, it destroys docks, warehouses, streets, and buildings. Sometimes, large fishing boats will be carried away and grounded hundreds of feet from their moorings. Most of all, the floodwater will drown virtually all who get in its way.

These waves were once especially deadly because they could not be predicted. An earthquake near Chile could cause a tsunami in Hawaii. Japan has been a particular target of these giant waves, and, in fact, the word *tsunami* is Japanese. Translated literally, it means "harbor wave." Many of the tsunamis that hit Japan form in the country's natural harbors.

Before predictions could be made, the first indication most people had that a tsunami was coming was when the ocean seemed to fall away from the seashore. This effect would happen as the force of the tsunami built a giant wave. By the time this occurred, it was almost too late to escape. Tsunamis move very fast. Anyone close enough to see the ocean "run away" will most likely be killed by the wave.

Improvements in earthquake monitoring and the advent of international communication have robbed tsunamis of much of their surprise. Detection of undersea earthquakes has allowed scientists to predict when and where tsunamis will strike. In the Pacific Ocean, a network of wave watchers has been set up with a center in Honolulu, Hawaii. The Tsunami Warning System receives information on all earthquakes that take place in and around the Pacific. Its scientists issue an area-wide warning if they think a tsunami has been formed. This advance notice can give people enough time to flee to higher ground.

Earthquakes

An earthquake is caused when rock snaps forward or breaks along a line called a fault. The slipping or breaking

Underwater earthquakes can cause huge sea waves called tsunamis. These boats and cars were destroyed by a tsunami off the coast of Alaska.

TYPES OF SEISMIC WAVES

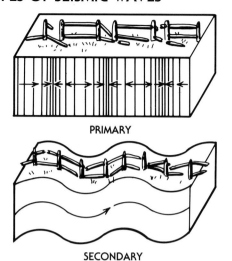

PRIMARY

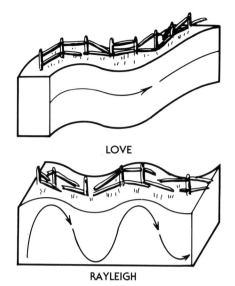

LOVE

SECONDARY

RAYLEIGH

An earthquake's destructive power comes from the seismic waves that shake the ground. Scientists identify four different patterns of seismic waves. These patterns can be seen in the way the waves move the land.

Primary waves are the first waves detected by seismometers. That is because they travel the fastest, and because they travel in a straight line, alternately pushing and then pulling the ground like an accordion.

Secondary waves travel slightly slower than primary waves, but they cause greater damage. That is because they move in an "s" pattern, causing the ground both to ripple up and down and shake from side to side. This shakes buildings and cracks their foundations.

Love waves travel near the surface, so they, too, are very destructive. Their wave pattern is horizontal, and they often bend or twist railroad tracks, roads, and bridges.

Rayleigh waves, like Love waves, are named after the scientist who discovered them. Also like Love waves, they travel near the surface. Since their pattern is up and down, they churn the top layer of land just like an ocean breaker churns the top layer of water.

can take place for miles along the fault. It can also go deep underground. To simplify their studies, scientists measure earthquakes from the underground area where the most movement takes place. This area is called the focus. The point on the ground above the focus is called the epicenter.

An earthquake sends out waves of energy through the ground. Some of these waves—which are called seismic waves—can travel thousands of miles through the earth. They can be detected by seismometers on the other side of the world. Naturally, a very powerful earthquake will send waves farther than a quake that merely rattles a few windows.

There are four kinds of seismic waves—primary, secondary, Love, and Rayleigh. Primary and secondary waves are the first to be recorded by seis-

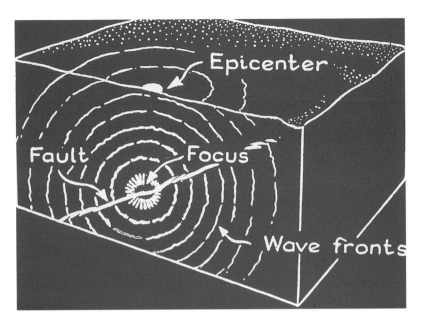

This diagram shows an earthquake moving out from the focus.

mometers. They travel deep underground. Love and Rayleigh waves travel near the surface.

Primary waves push rock together and pull it apart as they travel away from the focus. On the surface, the waves pull apart fences or telephone lines. Secondary waves are slightly slower than primary waves. They shake the ground horizontally and vertically, as a bucking bronco shakes its rider. Of the four seismic waves, secondary waves hit building foundations the hardest. During an earthquake, they cause most of the damage to man-made structures.

The two slower types of seismic waves—Love waves and Rayleigh waves, named after the scientists who discovered them—travel near the surface of the ground. Love waves shake the ground from side to side. They often bend railroad tracks out of shape during a large earthquake. Rayleigh waves travel through the ground like breaking waves along a seacoast. They move the

ground up, forward, down, and back in an elliptical pattern. They cause damage similar to that caused by secondary waves.

Earthquakes happen too fast for most people to tell the difference between one type of wave and another. The only way to tell them apart is to record the quake on a seismograph, which detects and records each wave separately. Even so, seismologists can have a hard time separating one wave recording from another if the earthquake has been particularly violent.

Living with earthquakes is part of living on a tectonically active planet. And human beings have been living with the destruction they cause almost since the human race began. The side effects of plate tectonics are not all bad for humans, however. In fact, the earth's continents and most human civilizations would not have come into existence had it not been for another side effect—volcanoes.

Explaining and Predicting Volcanic Eruptions

Volcanoes, like earthquakes, were once explained by ancient myths and religious beliefs. Many people around the world considered volcanoes to be the homes of gods. Natives of the Polynesian Islands of the South Pacific, for example, once thought volcanoes marked sites of battles between the fire goddess Pele and her sister Namakaokahai.

The word *volcano* itself comes from Roman mythology. There is a volcanic island that lies off the coast of Sicily in the Mediterranean Sea. It was named Vulcano in the belief that its smoke and fire came from the forge of Vulcan, the god of fire and metalworking. The original word for the study of volcanoes, *vulcanology*, also comes from this ancient myth. The word is now spelled *volcanology*.

A volcano is simply a hole in the ground that lets molten rock, or lava, flow over the earth's surface. This is the way the earth makes new surface land. Depending on how it cools, lava becomes different types of rock—granite, schist, and so on. Erosion of these rocks into sediment leads to the creation of

Volcanic explosions, like earthquakes, mystified early civilizations. Here, a cinder cone erupts in 1971 in western Nicaragua.

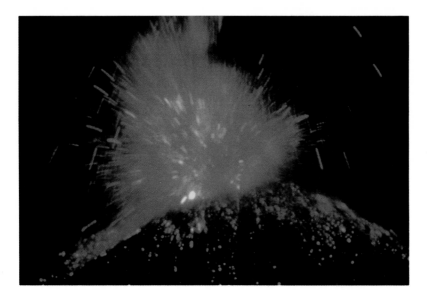

Early scientists could not easily study volcanoes and considered them unimportant. This spectacular view of a volcano in central Mexico shows lava bursting far above the crater rim.

other rock types, such as sandstone. Lava is also rich in minerals like iron and nitrogen that help plants grow. As the lava erodes, these nutrients become part of the surrounding soil. Farmers like to plant crops on or near volcanoes to take advantage of this excellent natural fertilizer. In Italy, for example, no matter how many times Mount Vesuvius has erupted, farmers have kept returning to their farms on its slopes.

Melting Plates and Rings of Fire

Until the discovery of plate tectonics, most scientists thought volcanoes were geologically unimportant nuisances. Aristotle considered volcanoes to be diseases of the earth, much like boils on a human being. Later, scientists thought volcanoes were the result of natural gas exploding within the earth. But for the most part, scientists ignored volcanoes. They could not realistically study them. No one could dig into a volcano and discover how it worked. And no one was

interested anyway because volcanoes did nothing more than throw out ash and lava, according to most scientists.

Plate tectonics, however, showed how volcanoes relate to the rest of the earth. Volcanoes form in three different ways. A few form along the world's rift zones, where magma seeps up and replaces seafloor that spreads from the rifts. Such volcanoes are created on the slopes of the ocean ridges that face away from the rifts. The seeping magma forms volcanic islands, huge mountains

A line of cinder cones in various stages of activity in Hawaii, 1983.

The Hawaiian Island volcanoes are the most well-known examples of volcanoes that form over hot spots in the earth's mantle. This Hawaiian volcano is the tallest known active volcano in the world.

large deposits of uranium or other radioactive materials. These deposits act like huge nuclear reactors, generating intense amounts of heat.

Hot spots can form volcanoes on land and in the middle of an ocean. As a plate passes over one of these areas, the superhot magma burns through points where the rock is thinnest. The Hawaiian Islands are the most widely known example of a hot spot at work. For millions of years, this hot spot has been burning holes through thin areas of the Pacific Plate. Each time it has burned through the plate, it has formed a new volcanic island. These extinct volcanoes formed a chain as they were carried away by plate movement. Only the island of Hawaii, after which this chain is named, has any active volcanoes—Mauna Loa and Kilauea.

The most active and violent volcanoes, however, are those formed near

A fountain of lava shoots high in the air during a volcanic eruption in Hawaii, 1959. A calderan volcano, the cone completely collapsed after the eruption and formed a lake one hundred meters deep and one kilometer in diameter.

that poke above the waves. Some of these islands are flattened by wind and wave action, forming the guyots that Harold Hess discovered. Not all of these volcanoes have disappeared, however. Iceland, which straddles the Mid-Atlantic Ridge, was created by volcanoes that formed in the ridge. The land itself is mostly lava that the volcanoes have shot out over the centuries.

Less frequently, volcanoes also form over "hot spots" in the earth's mantle. Hot spots are isolated areas where the magma is far hotter than elsewhere in the mantle. Scientists are not sure why these areas are so hot. The most likely explanation is that these areas contain the world's subduction trenches, where one plate dives under another. As a plate dives into the earth, it begins to melt. The surface of these plates is a combination of basalt, ocean sediments, and seawater. This mixture melts more rapidly than the rest of the plate, which is made of basalt. The plate does not have to get too deep for the seafloor surface to start melting and combining with the magma. The resulting magma mix is lighter than the purer magma around it. And like oil in water, it rises to the top of the mantle.

The lighter magma usually forms under a continent, where the rock is less dense than under the seafloor. It can also be carried under a section of the overthrusting plate that has been fractured and weakened by the pressures of subduction. In either case, the magma seeps up and melts out a chamber in the rock, where it is joined by still more magma rising from the melting plate. As the pressure in this chamber increases, the magma is forced up through cracks

Basalt lava erupts from Kilauea's East Rift volcano in Hawaii.

in the rock until it comes out on the earth's surface. At this point, the magma is known as lava. The lava usually forms a volcano. Sometimes, it simply seeps out of the ground in a lava flow covering thousands of miles.

The Japanese, Indonesian, and Aleu-

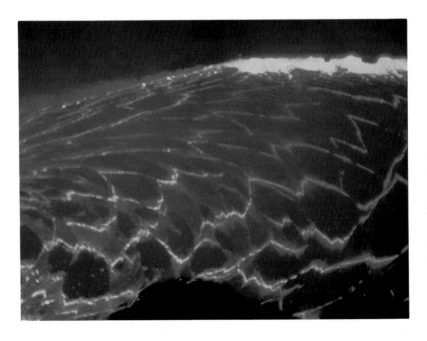

Motion of lava beneath the surface causes the cooled skin on the surface to break apart, revealing the hotter material beneath. On a small scale, these sections of cooled skin above molten material duplicate the motion of the earth's plates as they move above the mantle.

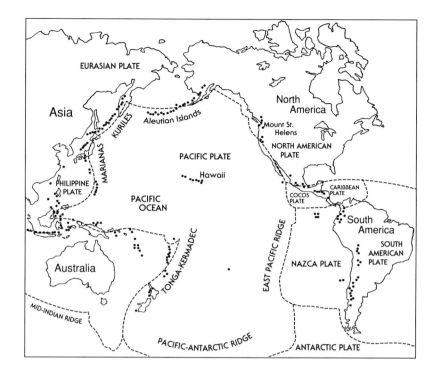

The dots on this map show the locations of active volcanoes in the Pacific Ocean area of earth. Almost all active volcanoes occur at the margins of large, moving blocks of earth's crust.

tian islands were all created by volcanoes arising at the edge of Pacific Ocean subduction zones. They are part of a geologic phenomenon called the Ring of Fire. The ring is a chain of volcanoes that circles the Pacific. Other names for the ring are the Andesite Line and the Continental Margin Chain.

About 180 volcanoes make up the Ring of Fire. They stretch north from the Philippines through Japan to the Aleutian Islands, a string of volcanic islands that lead away from the southwest corner of Alaska. The ring continues along the Alaskan coast and south through the volcanic Cascade Mountains of North America. The chain then heads through Mexico, Central America, and South America, where it helps form the Andes Mountains. There the ring turns west and goes through New Zealand, then into the East Indies, where it bends north and returns to the Philippines.

The Ring of Fire has hosted some

of the world's most devastating eruptions. The worst volcanic eruption in the past two hundred years occurred in 1883. Krakatau was a volcanic island in the East Indies. In 1883, it virtually destroyed itself in an explosion three thousand times more powerful than the atomic bomb that destroyed Hiroshima during World War II. The force of the explosion created giant waves. These waves spread out in a circle two hundred miles wide and killed more than thirty-six thousand people. The burst of pressure created by the explosion was recorded on scientific instruments around the world. The sound of the eruption was heard more than three thousand miles away. Pieces of the pulverized island itself tinged the sky red around the world for years after the explosion.

Recent volcanic eruptions have not been as devastating as the one that blew up Krakatau. But they have claimed

Located in the Sunda Strait between Sumatra and Java, Krakatau is famous for its devastating 1883 eruption, the largest in recorded history.

Starting on March 27, 1980, a series of steam and ash eruptions blew the top off the mountain. These eruptions created a crater that faced to the north. Swarms of earthquakes shook the mountain's slopes and the surrounding countryside. On May 18, an earthquake shattered the north slope, starting an avalanche of rock and debris. The landslide provided a sudden release of pressure that had been built up by the lava and gases underground. This material exploded out of the north side of the mountain.

Like steam jetting from a broken valve, a gigantic mass of lava, gases, ash, and earth exploded up and out. The force of the blast knocked down trees for miles. A huge flow of boiling mud covered the land to the north of the mountain. The ash blew high into the air and drifted hundreds of miles, cov-

newspaper headlines around the world for the death and destruction they have caused. The 1980 eruption of Mount Saint Helens in southwestern Washington state, in particular, received much attention. Mount Saint Helens is part of the Cascade mountain range, which sweeps down through Washington, Oregon, and part of northern California.

Mount Saint Helens had not erupted for more than 120 years. Throughout the world, people admired it for its beauty and symmetry. The residents of nearby towns had grown accustomed to its gentle, snowcapped slopes. And many considered it the American equivalent of Japan's Mount Fuji, itself a beautiful volcanic mountain.

The eruption of Mount Saint Helens in Washington on July 22, 1980. The volcano had not erupted in more than 120 years.

ering the ground as far away as Idaho. Seventy people and more than twelve million animals, birds, and fish were killed.

Not all volcanic eruptions have to be spectacular to be deadly. In 1985, the Nevado del Ruiz volcano in Colombia had a minor eruption. The heat from the eruption was enough to melt a small portion of the ice and snow at its peak. The meltwater then rushed down the slopes of the volcano, gathering dirt and debris into a 130-foot-high mudflow. The flow killed twenty-three thousand people before it stopped and buried the agricultural center of Armero.

Scientists had known that the volcano was about to have some sort of eruption. They had been monitoring earthquakes caused by magma shifting in the volcano for at least a year before the eruption. The mountain had also been venting clouds of sulfur, an indication that an eruption might occur. A team of scientists even recommended evacuating Armero eight hours before the mudflow buried the town. But local officials ignored the warnings. The town's churches and radio station even broadcast messages urging people not to panic or leave town.

Hope for Future Predictions

As with earthquakes, no one can say for sure if a volcano is going to erupt or not. In the past few years, Mount Saint Helens has had a number of small eruptions. This activity may mean the mountain is getting ready for another large eruption.

Even though the volcanic eruption in Nevado del Ruiz, Colombia, was minor, it had devastating results. The heat from the eruption melted the ice and snow at its peak, triggering debris flows that swept down river valleys and overran villages.

But scientists do have a better understanding about how volcanoes work. Scientists know that volcanoes are connected systems created by the moving plates of the earth. And, most important, they now have new tools to find out what happens before these fiery mountains explode.

As the disaster in Colombia showed, scientists can come closer to predicting volcanic eruptions than they can to forecasting earthquakes. Before they erupt, volcanoes often send out great clouds of gases, ash, steam, or smoke. They send out measurable seismic waves that signal the increased pressure of magma on the surrounding rock. These waves can also signal a buildup of heat that has melted snow and ice on a volcano's summit. This meltwater can lubricate the underlying rock and allow it to move freely. The shape of the volcano itself can tell how much of a danger it poses. A tall, well-shaped volcanic mountain has undoubtedly erupted within a few hundred years. But a volcano whose sides have worn away to a core of ancient lava probably died out hundreds of thousands of years ago.

A new type of observation may play a role in predicting future eruptions. In

Before they erupt, volcanoes typically spew out great clouds of gas, ash, steam, or smoke.

the two years before a Costa Rica volcano erupted in 1989, geophysicists Geoff Brown and Helen Rymer recorded a change in the planet's gravity, the force that pulls two items together and holds objects on the earth. Nobody knows for sure what causes gravity. Scientists do know, however, that the strength of this force depends on how

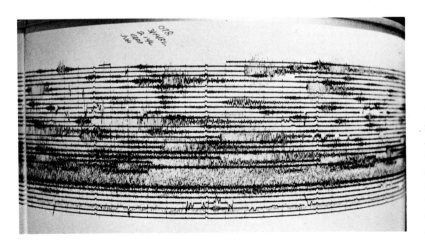

The dark unlined area recorded on this seismograph at the U.S. Geological Survey office in Vancouver records extensive ground movement after the eruption of Mount Saint Helens.

Mount Saint Helens spews steam and ash before its eruption in 1980. Signs such as these help scientists predict when a volcano is likely to erupt.

dense each item is. Two pennies resting on a table do not move toward each other because they are too small to exert much force. But they stay on the table because the earth is big enough to exert a great force over them.

Mountains and other large landforms can distort the earth's own gravity slightly. A heavy mass of lava inside a volcano can also affect gravity. Scientists have measured both gains and losses in gravity at different volcanoes before eruption. They think the increase comes from dense lava forcing its way into the volcano, creating more of a pull on the surrounding area. Such a buildup occurs before most volcanoes erupt. Scientists may be able to use measurements of the increase in gravity to predict future eruptions.

As scientists continue to refine their techniques and gather more information about volcanoes in the years to come, they will form an even clearer picture of what goes on inside and beneath volcanic systems. With this information, they hope to have a better chance of warning people of coming volcanic devastation.

Volcanic Types

A volcano is a hole, or vent, in the crust of the earth surrounded by a hill or a mountain made of hardened lava. Volcanoes have many shapes, depending on what type of lava they spew out. The most common varieties are:

Plinian—These volcanoes get their

Researchers seem to sit in a sea of lava as they study a volcanic eruption.

name from Pliny the Elder, a Roman historian who died in the eruption of Mount Vesuvius in A.D. 79. A Plinian volcano is formed by thick, sticky lava flowing out of the ground and creating a cone-shaped mountain. Between eruptions, the lava forms a thick plug over the volcano's central vent. A typical Plinian eruption starts with an explosion as the pressure of rising lava blows out the old plug. Tons of rocks, dust, and ash shoot thousands of feet into the air. The explosion usually leaves a crater at the top of the volcano. After the explosion, lava flows out of the crater and down the sides of the volcano.

Strombolian—These volcanoes are named after the Italian island of Stromboli, where they were first described. The lava that forms this volcano is thinner than that of a Plinian volcano. In a Strombolian eruption, the volcano shoots out round blobs of lava called volcanic bombs or volcanic splatter. It also vents tall clouds of white steam, cre-

Volcanoes come in many different shapes. This volcano in New Zealand has an almost perfect cone. This view shows a steam eruption in 1968. Ash has darkened a fresh layer of snow at the summit.

FIVE MAJOR TYPES OF VOLCANOES

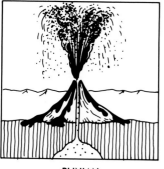

PLINIAN

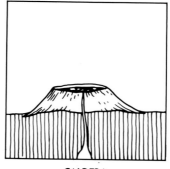

CALDERA

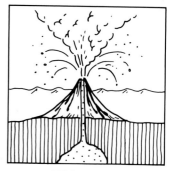

STROMBOLIAN

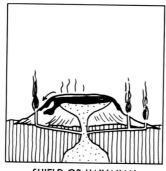

SHIELD OR HAWAIIAN

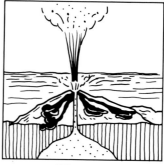

SUBMARINE

Plinian. A cone-shaped mountain is formed by quick, violent eruptions. Between eruptions, thick, sticky lava forms a hard plug over the volcano's central vent. Magma underneath builds up pressure and blows out this plug, resulting in an explosion that shoots tons of rocks, dust, and ash thousands of feet into the air, leaving a large crater.

Caldera. A caldera is a huge crater or depression in the earth where a volcanic mountain once stood. It is formed by a particularly violent Plinian eruption. This releases so much magma that when the eruption is over, there is not enough magma built up inside the cone to hold up its massive walls. As a result, the cone collapses, forming a wide, circular depression.

Strombolian. Formed by longer, less violent eruptions than Plinian volcanoes,

Strombolian volcanoes often produce extremely tall mountains. An eruption may last several years, during which time blobs of lava, or volcanic splatter, and plumes of white steam spew from the crater, and thin lava flows down the sides of the mountain.

Shield or Hawaiian. The cone is a low, broadly sloping hill that looks like a shield. This is formed by thin, runny lava that spreads out over the land. During an eruption the thin lava sprays up like a curtain of lava.

Submarine. An underwater volcano. Lava from an eruption cools as soon as it touches the surrounding water, forming short, rounded "pillows" of lava. A submarine volcano may eventually pile up enough pillow lava to become an island. If still active then, it will likely become a shield volcano.

Incandescent lava is hurled above the volcanic rim of this volcano in Stromboli, Italy. All volcanoes that hurl this type of lava are known as Strombolian, after the volcanoes on this unique island.

ated as underground water leaks into the volcano's central vent. While Plinian eruptions are usually quick and violent, Strombolian eruptions can last for centuries.

Shield or Hawaiian—These volcanoes are made from thin, runny lava that spreads out over the land or seafloor. When it hardens, the lava forms a low, broadly sloping cone that looks like a warrior's shield. The lava is thin enough to spray upward out of cracks leading away from the vent. This action creates the effect of a "curtain" of lava coming out of the ground.

Submarine—Submarine volcanoes are underwater and do not form as their land-based counterparts do. Lava coming out of a submarine vent cools as soon as it touches the surrounding water. It cools into short, rounded clumps that scientists call "pillows." If the vent stays open long enough, this pillow lava will pile up and, eventually, form an island. Often, sea-based shield volcanoes will start this way.

Caldera—A caldera is the remnant of a volcano that has collapsed in on itself. Some large volcanoes have chambers of lava inside their cones. These chambers are filled from the volcano's main magma chamber far beneath the ground, and they help support the weight of the volcano's cone. Occasionally, one of these volcanoes will empty its chambers before fresh lava can fill them. Soon after the eruption, the walls of the volcano will collapse into the empty chambers. All that will be left of the mountain is a wide, bowl-shaped depression in the earth. This depression is called a caldera.

Building to Last

The enormous growth in earth's human population over the centuries makes the issue of plate tectonics more important than ever before. More people are located today in areas where they can be hurt, or even killed, by the action of plate tectonics. And they are being forced to come up with ways to minimize the destruction that the movement of earth's plates can cause.

Earthquake Damage

Of the earth's geologic forces, earthquakes cause the most total damage to humanity. Tens of thousands of people die each year, and millions of dollars' worth of homes, office buildings, freeways, and other structures are destroyed. If a city is lucky, it will not suffer further devastation from fires caused by ruptured gas lines or overturned stoves.

It is not the shaking of the ground that causes most of the deaths and injuries during an earthquake. A person standing alone in the middle of a field might be thrown to the ground and bruised, but that is the worst damage he or she would feel. The real devastation comes from collapsing buildings, freeway overpasses, and other structures that are twisted and shaken apart as the ground below them moves. For the past three decades, architects have been trying to design buildings that can withstand earthquakes.

In 1988, an earthquake in the Soviet

On December 7, 1988, a large earthquake hit the republic of Armenia. Badly constructed buildings, made up of concrete slabs, collapsed under the pressure, turning whole cities into masses of rubble.

Union's republic of Armenia showed how dangerous buildings that are not earthquake-safe can be. Armenia lies to the northeast of Turkey between the Black Sea and the Caspian Sea. It also lies near the tectonic border where the Arabian Plate dives beneath the Eurasian Plate. The tectonic activity in this area has created many faults throughout Armenia and other nearby countries. On December 7, a large earthquake struck western Armenia. People living more

This aerial view shows a rupture in the earth about thirty kilometers long. The rupture occurred after a 6.8 earthquake in Meckering, Australia.

than one hundred miles away from the quake's epicenter felt its effects.

The towns and villages of Armenia were filled with badly constructed buildings. Almost none of them survived the disaster. Many houses were built of hardened mud bricks held together with more mud. Insulation was provided by ceilings made of rock. The country's newer offices, schools, and apartment buildings were also poorly constructed to survive an earthquake. Most of these buildings were made up of concrete slabs stacked on top of each other like metal shelves. And in most of them, the floors and walls were very loosely connected.

When the earthquake hit, these buildings immediately collapsed. A Soviet newspaper described them as falling apart like piles of matchboxes. In the city of Leninaken, the staircases in the Polytechnic Institute crumbled and fell. Those students who did not die in the fall were crushed to death under the weight of the stairs. Similar tragedies occurred throughout the area.

In Leninaken and other cities, the collapse of homes and buildings also broke open pipes carrying heating fuel. Fuel leaking from these pipes was ignited by overturned stoves and downed electrical wires. People were soon choking on smoke and fumes from fires throughout the cities. Many of the people who were still alive but trapped inside collapsed buildings died from smoke inhalation once the fires started.

In all, more than fifty thousand people died as a result of the earthquake. Only half the buildings in Leninaken were left standing. A Soviet news broadcast said Spitak, a town near Leninaken, had all but "been erased from the face of the earth." More than half a million people had lost their homes.

Riding Out Earthquakes

In an earthquake, buildings move back and forth with the seismic waves. This movement causes most of the structural damage to buildings. Neighboring buildings can slam into each other if they sway far enough to the side. A high rise can fracture at its base if it is connected to a long, low entry building. The strength and speed of these vibrations depends mostly on what type of ground the buildings are on.

It is better to build on solid rock than on soil or clay. Solid rock moves less in an earthquake. Seismic waves travel through it fairly quickly. They make the ground shiver rather than sway back and forth. A rock base makes it easier for architects to design buildings that will not shake apart or topple over during a large quake. In many areas, it is easy to build on or anchor a building to solid rock. Builders can even sink bolts through a building's frame to the underlying bedrock.

Still, building on bedrock has some risks. A rigid building set on solid rock can be shaken apart in an earthquake. An inflexible structure cannot withstand the short, sharp jolts. So architects design their buildings to sway slightly with the ground. The swaying turns the building into a giant spring that absorbs the force of the earthquake. The swaying also prevents walls and windows from shattering.

Loose soil, or ground that is made up of compacted soil and clay, is much more dangerous. This type of ground intensifies the effects of seismic waves. It converts sharp tremors into slow, rolling movements that rock the buildings above. This gentle rocking ends up whipping the buildings back and forth. The buildings twist out of shape and collapse.

To combat this effect, architects use techniques opposite to ones they use when building on solid rock. They make their structures more rigid. The best buildings for sediments are short and boxlike. They are designed to move as a

Made of fill dirt, this hillside collapsed during an earthquake in Berkeley, California, causing 121 meters of railroad track to slide down the hill.

Soil liquefaction and poor foundations caused whole apartment houses to lean and some to collapse in Niigata, Japan, 1964.

single unit on the swaying soil. In less rigid buildings, different parts can sway at different speeds. These individual actions can twist and tear the building apart.

During an earthquake, some loose or compacted soil goes through a pro-cess scientists call liquefaction. The seismic waves shake up the soil so much that it acts like a liquid. This happened in San Francisco during the 1989 earthquake. One district of the city was built on soil and loose rock or dirt that had been used to fill in a swampy area of the shore of San Francisco Bay. Though the land had seemed solid enough to build on, the earthquake rapidly softened it. Buildings collapsed as the ground flowed away and their foundations sank. In some areas, potholes opened up in streets and parking lots as the soil underneath settled. The city government kept many people from going back into their homes for fear the houses would collapse from the extra weight of their bodies.

Another example of liquefaction occurred during Alaska's Good Friday earthquake in 1964. The southern coast of Alaska marks the boundary where part of the Pacific Plate slides under a piece of the North American Plate. On March 27 of that year, a segment of the Pacific Plate snapped forward a few feet. It caused a huge earthquake that devas-

An entire subdivision in Anchorage, Alaska was destroyed when soil liquefied during an earthquake. Sand and clay soils weakened and moved down the slope in a complicated motion.

tated Anchorage and destroyed much of the town of Valdez. Part of the damage in Anchorage was caused in the city's Turnagain Heights area. This neighborhood was built on a seventy-foot-high bluff just above the seashore. When the quake hit, the sand, gravel, and clay that made up the mound shook loose and flowed down past the shoreline. Though few people were killed (the whole earthquake took only one hundred lives), the neighborhood was destroyed.

Secondary Damage

A big concern among builders and government officials is the damage that occurs when buildings knock into each other during an earthquake. Buildings set next to each other cannot help but collide when they are shaken by an earthquake. The buildings knock pieces off each other and break open. New buildings in earthquake-prone areas are built far enough apart to keep this type of damage from happening. But older buildings that were built before the enforcement of earthquake safety guidelines are still a hazard.

The interior of a building can be dangerous even if the building itself is built to be earthquake-safe. Bookcases and computer banks can fall over onto people. Boilers and other machinery can break loose and bounce around. Doors can jam shut if their frames bend out of shape, trapping people in their rooms or offices. This type of secondary damage can injure or kill people even if the building does not collapse.

Architects have started fighting these dangers by using combinations of rigid and flexible supports. Whenever possible, they try to anchor homes and smaller buildings to strong foundations of bedrock to reduce the force of vibrations. They reinforce walls with rods of steel. They try to design gaps throughout the building so that it can bend

These foundation supports reinforce the brick walls of this building. Architects hope these reinforcements will help buildings withstand earthquakes.

without breaking apart. Taller buildings contain specially reinforced joints to let them sway gently without collapsing. Scientists and builders have also started using laboratory-tested "bumpers" of steel and rubber that are placed around the foundation supports of buildings. They hope these will absorb ground vibrations.

Creeping Land

As the tectonic plates move, they pull apart the continents that rest on top of them. This is a very slow activity. At its fastest, it moves at a speed of a couple of inches a year. But it is fast enough to cause problems for some people who live where the land is tearing.

The San Andreas Fault is the boundary line between the Pacific and the North American plates. A person standing on the North American Plate long enough would see part of Southern California traveling to the northwest. Over the years, many landforms have been

Along the San Andreas Fault, many landforms have been displaced. (above) A stream bed is moved out of line by the fault's movements. (left) Rows in a cultivated field in Guatemala are bent by the effects of an earthquake.

This drain at the Almaden Winery in California has been offset by the movement along the San Andreas Fault.

displaced along the fault. Streambeds are moved out of line. Hills break in two, one half seeming to sidestep away from the other. This process is called fault creep. It is becoming a nuisance to the people who live along the fault.

In California's Napa Valley, for example, a winery was built near the fault. Unknown to the winery's owners, a branch of the fault ran right under their land. Over the years, one side of this fault has followed the Pacific Plate northward. As it moves, it carries along the part of a winery warehouse that crossed the fault line. The building is slowly being torn apart by this unforeseen ground movement. At the same time, the fault is displacing part of a vineyard that was planted nearby.

The fault creates similar problems throughout the state. County roads that cross the fault are wrenched apart and have to be rebuilt. Drainage ditches have to be repaired every few years. And buildings unlucky enough to be built across the fault eventually will be torn down.

Plate Tectonics and Natural Resources

Plate tectonics deserves at least part of the credit for the world's supply of natural resources. The constant alteration of the earth's surface has created accessible pockets of oil and minerals. If not for plate tectonics, many of these materials would be buried deep in the crust. Human beings would not be able to mine and use them.

The benefits of plate tectonics take a long time to accumulate. Oil does not form overnight. Volcanic activity must die down before miners can harvest earth's minerals and precious metals. Many of these treasures are still unreachable, at least with today's technol-ogy. But understanding how they are created helps scientists locate other available deposits.

Earth and Oil

Oil is the end product of the decay of plant and animal matter. It is a sludge of debris that forms underground. It takes millions of years for oil to form. It can be created only under very precise conditions. And it must be trapped in a certain way before people can pump it out of the ground.

Scientists who study oil do not know

Oil can be brought to the surface by underground pressure. The La Brea Tar Pits in Los Angeles, California, are an example of these surface pools. Hundreds of bones of prehistoric animals have been found in the pools.

PLATE TECTONICS AND OIL DEPOSITS

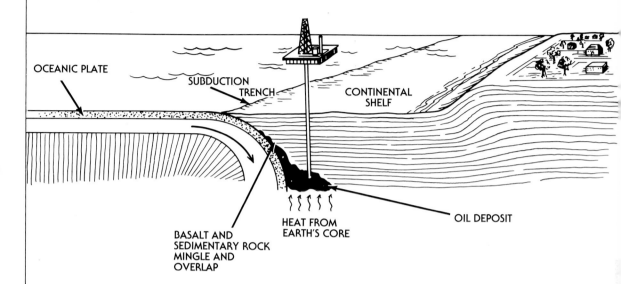

OCEANIC PLATE

SUBDUCTION
TRENCH

CONTINENTAL
SHELF

BASALT AND
SEDIMENTARY ROCK
MINGLE AND
OVERLAP

HEAT FROM
EARTH'S CORE

OIL DEPOSIT

It takes millions of years and very special conditions for oil to be created. One of the ideal places to find these conditions is along a subduction trench, where the ocean floor dives below a continental shelf. For example, when North America and Europe drifted apart to form the Atlantic Ocean, new continental shelves, or sloping layers of sediment, were formed off the new coastlines. These shelves collected large quantities of microscopic plant and animal remains.

The breakup of the continents also caused numerous landslides. These covered the new organic deposits quickly, before they could decompose. Pockets of the rich organic deposits were then trapped near the subduction trenches, where oceanic plates of heavy basaltic rock converge with the sedimentary continental shelves. There, heat from the melting rock beneath the trenches helped "cook" the organic deposits into oil.

exactly how long it takes the earth to make it. They think the process takes at least a few million years, since it depends on a couple of long-term geologic events. The first of these events is the formation of a geologic basin, a large, bowl-shaped depression in the ground. It can be the floor of a lake or the bottom of a very young ocean. A basin can be formed by plates pulling apart from one another in the early development of a rift zone. It can also be formed by plate action making continental rock sink.

Microscopic plants and animals die and settle to the bottom of the basin. Usually, these plants and animals collect under a cover of oxygen-poor water. If the water contains a lot of oxygen, bacteria will grow uncontrollably and will eat the plant and animal tissue before it can turn into oil.

As this organic matter collects, it becomes covered by a thick layer of sediment. The sediment protects it from being eaten by the bacteria that are able to survive in the oxygen-poor water. Scientists think the sediments come from sudden floods or landslides. The normal deposit of sediment from erosion is too slow to preserve the material.

Under the sediment, the organic matter starts to decay into a slimy ooze called kerogen. As the sediment thickens, the temperature of the kerogen starts to rise. The gradual heating is caused by the warmth of the earth. It is aided by the heat the kerogen itself gives off as it decays.

Heating is the most tricky part of the process. If the kerogen is not heated enough, it will not change into oil. If it gets too hot, it will decompose into graphite, methane, and other elements.

The mass must cook in a range of 60 to 150°C, which is about 150 to 250°F.

As it cooks, the kerogen slowly turns into crude oil. Scientists are trying to figure out exactly how this happens. All they know is that after an unknown length of time, the organic matter liquifies and changes into oil. The oil gets less thick and more valuable the longer it cooks. Lighter oil is easier to refine. This process that makes oil also produces natural gas at the same time. The lighter the oil, the more gas is formed.

Eventually, ground pressure forces the oil toward the surface. It continues upward until it reaches the surface or is trapped by rocks. Oil that reaches the surface forms pools that evaporate and are eaten by bacteria. Surface oil also forms traps for animals. The most famous of these traps is the La Brea Tar Pits in Los Angeles, California. There, scientists have pulled up the bones of hundreds of animals and one human

An offshore oil rig drills for oil off the coast of Massachusetts.

woman that sank into the pits.

To survive, oil needs a thick, dense cover to protect it from bacteria and evaporation. The shape of the ground can provide this protection. Oil deposits are often found in the tops of hill-shaped folds in the ground called anticlines. Sometimes, the anticlines actually form hills, though they can be buried by floods or landslides. Oil rises through the rock and soil layers of the anticline until it comes to a layer it cannot pass through. The oil will then form a big underground pool in the anticline.

An anticline is an example of a type of natural oil trap called a structural trap. Another common structural trap is called a salt dome. Salt, like oil, is another natural product of the earth. Occasionally, rock and sediment will build up around huge blocks of salt. Oil rising through these layers cannot pass through the plug of salt in its path. It pools under and around the salt.

Another kind of trap, called a stratigraphic trap, collects oil usually by holding the oil in an area where loose rock is surrounded by more firmly packed rock. One sort of stratigraphic trap uses fossilized sand bars called marine bar sandstone lenses to halt the flow of oil. These lenses absorb any oil that tries to flow through them.

Finding Oil

Petroleum geologists are scientists who specialize in looking for oil deposits. They analyze an area's landscape for telltale signs of oil traps. They look for obvious anticlines. They try to find areas that contain sedimentary basins. They take log-shaped samples of earth

An oil rig is towed to sea for use in Europe's North Sea.

and rock called core samples to see how the ground is shaped. When they find a likely area, they drill test wells to see if they can hit an oil deposit.

Studies in plate tectonics have aided petroleum geologists in their search for fresh oil reserves. Scientists have made maps of the way the earth's surface looked at different times. Geologists have used these maps to identify areas where kerogen may have formed. Other scientists have used satellites to find huge depressions in the ground that mark former geologic basins. Often, these depressions are too wide and too shallow for people on the ground to see.

The rise in offshore drilling is one outcome of applying plate tectonic knowledge to oil exploration. The Atlantic Ocean was originally a series of sedimentary basins. The first basin formed when North America split from what is now Europe. A second basin was created as South America separated from Africa. Conditions in these areas were ideal for oil formation. The basins were rich in microscopic plant and animal life. Probably many landslides happened as the continents pulled apart. And heat from the developing Mid-Atlantic Ridge would have been enough to start cooking the kerogen. Today, oil rigs in the middle of Europe's North Sea have tapped some of the oil deposits formed in these basins.

The Gulf of Mexico is another area of undersea geologic basins. Mexico's Pemex oil company operates oil-drlling platforms that have been there since the 1900s. And Costa Rica's national oil company, RECOPE, had an outside firm study its east and west coastlines. Costa Rica, a country in Central America, lies at the western end of the Caribbean Plate. Just off the western shore, a small plate called the Cocos Plate dives under Central America. Over time, geologic basins formed and filled with sediment on both coasts. The RECOPE study

showed that some oil has formed in these basins. Whether enough oil exists to make mining it profitable remains to be seen.

Volcanic Mineral Wealth

The island of Cyprus lies near the boundary where the African Plate is diving beneath the Eurasian Plate. It was created by lava flowing up from the melting African Plate. The rock that formed the island contained huge quantities of copper, a metal valuable for making tools, jewelry, and weapons. Cyprus's copper deposits are some of the biggest in the world. They have been mined for thousands of years by many civilizations, including ancient Greece and Rome. The Greeks even named the island using their word for "copper."

For a long time, scientists thought

Black smokers are underwater geysers that look like chimneys, spewing out black soot from fires beneath the seafloor.

Some of the material ejected from underwater geysers forms large balls of minerals. These balls of manganese oxide were formed in this way.

that the lava simply transported the metals and minerals from the planet's interior. In the 1970s, however, scientists studying ocean floors discovered underwater geysers that were rich in minerals, including copper. These geysers looked like underwater chimneys pouring out black soot from fires beneath the seafloor. Because the water in these geysers was so dark, scientists named them black smokers.

The mines of Cyprus and many other nations were once sites of black smokers. Old lava deposits near the mines contain tubes of minerals that formed around ancient black smokers while the island was being built. Knowledge of the mines' tectonic background is being used to find more deposits of valuable minerals. Geologists and prospectors alike are searching for signs of ancient black smokers. Knowing that a particular piece of land was once underwater helps them narrow their search.

A black smoker forms when seawa-

ter leaks down through cracks in the seafloor. As it meets a rising mass of magma, the water heats up into steam. The salt and other minerals already in the water pull metals and more minerals from the magma. The superhot, mineral-laden water and steam then jet back to the surface. When it reaches the bottom of the seafloor, it ejects the minerals into the water. The minerals flow out from the geyser and settle with volcanic and other sediments.

Present-day black smokers also form another type of mineral deposit that some countries are trying to mine. But these deposits cannot be mined in the typical way. Some of the material ejected from the underwater geysers forms large balls around bits of solid debris. These balls, or nodules, eventually get big enough to sink to the ocean's floor. There are areas of the world's oceans that are carpeted with thousands of these nodules. Many of them contain manganese, a fairly common mineral on land. They also can contain copper, cobalt, and other more valuable minerals. These minerals are scarce or hard to mine on land.

Currently, companies from a number of countries are bringing these nodules to the surface. The mid-Pacific is the main site of these mining efforts. Huge fields of nodules have been discovered on the seafloor, though the mining companies keep their locations secret. The more common mining methods involve dragging scoops or chains of buckets along the seafloor. Some companies have been experimenting with a type of vacuum that rolls along the sea floor like a tractor. But some people are questioning the wisdom of taking away these balls of minerals. They are concerned about

By tapping underwater geysers and hot springs, people have been able to harness the energy from the superheated water that is generated far beneath the surface of the earth.

the effect the absence of the nodules will have on the sea itself and the plants and animals that live in it. Right now, no one knows what will happen.

Natural Central Heating

The energy that creates black smokers and volcanoes comes from inside the earth. Scientists estimate that the planet's inside temperature is greater than four thousand degrees Celsius, or around ten thousand degrees Fahrenheit. Part of this heat was left over from the planet's creation billions of years ago. Scientists also think radioactive decay is helping to heat the crust and upper magma.

Much of this heat is inaccessible to people. Some of it lies far beneath the deepest ocean trenches. More is spread out through miles of continental crust. Quite a bit is given off by lava cooling after it gushes out of the world's volcanoes.

On the other hand, some of this heat can be tapped indirectly at the planet's tectonic edges. This heat is called geothermal energy. People have been using geothermal energy as an alternative to oil for the past few decades. They have done so by tapping into the geysers and hot springs that are created as water comes in contact with rising magma. This same process that creates black smokers also creates these geothermal vents. Seawater leaks down through cracks in the crust until it reaches deposits of magma or very hot rock. The water then flashes into steam and forces its way to the surface through other cracks in the ground. These cracks are called geothermal vents.

This high-pressure steam is used to generate electricity in cities around the world. Pipes carry the steam from the vents to generators in power plants. Half the power for the city of San Francisco is produced in a canyon ninety miles north of the city. This canyon is near the edge of the San Andreas Fault. It contains hundreds of geothermal vents that have been tapped to meet the city's growing power needs.

Iceland also uses geysers and hot springs for most of its energy needs. The people of Iceland do more than use geothermal power to turn electric generators. They pump out hot groundwater to heat their homes and businesses. Some of the springs are pure enough to pump the water directly to a home's hot water pipes. Before geothermal energy became a practical alternative, the people of Iceland burned coal or other fuels to keep warm. This method created clouds of soot and other pollutants that covered their cities. By using geothermal power, they have been able to clean up their skies.

Unfortunately, geothermal energy is not a perfect answer to the world's energy problems. People who use geothermal energy have come across a number of drawbacks. Like oil, geothermal energy is a limited resource. Pumping out too much of the superheated water can cause springs and geysers to dry up. This has already happened on one of the islands of New Zealand, where the inhabitants have been tapping some of its geothermal pools for years. Other pools that were sacred to the island's native people, the Maori, were left alone. Unfortunately, so much water was pumped out for private use that some of the Maori pools dried up as

In New Zealand, people have been tapping geothermal pools for years. In some cases, the pools have dried up from overuse.

well. The country's government tried to correct the situation by pumping water back into the ground. It had to stop when the increased pressure started a number of small earthquakes.

Another problem is that the geothermally heated water is often rich in minerals. Just as with black smokers, the heated water pulls minerals from surrounding rock and magma. Over the years, these minerals can clog pipes leading into homes and power plants. Some people have profited from the clogging by scraping out the minerals and selling them.

Finally, there are not enough geothermally active areas to supply power for the entire world. As technology improves, however, geothermal power may take up more of the burden of meeting humanity's power needs.

Charting Earth's Changing Face

The process of plate tectonics continues to carry the continents around the world. In a few million years, today's maps of earth will be useless. Most people do not have to worry about this because they will not be around to see the future earth. Still, scientists are interested in predicting what the earth will look like. They feel it will help them gain a better understanding of the way the plates move now. They have been putting together maps of the earth's past geography for the same reason.

Plate tectonics works so slowly that few people except scientists can tell it works at all. Earthquakes, volcanoes, and distorted landforms are the only easily seen evidence of plate movement. From year to year, a single plate may move only four inches. Yet over millions of years, the plates have changed the face of the globe many times.

Plotting Pangaea

Scientists studying the geologic record have shown that Alfred Wegener's continental drift theory was partly right. At one time, most of the world's land was combined in a single supercontinent. Wegener had proposed a continent like this in his book on continental drift. He called this land Pangaea, a name he made from Greek words meaning "all" and "land." Modern scientists call the supercontinent they found Pangaea as well.

Pangaea existed between 250 million and 300 million years ago. It was more or less centered over the equator. Pangaea itself was the product of hundreds of millions of years of previous plate tectonic action. (Scientists have tracked the movement of plates and continents to a time more than 500 million years before today.) The supercontinent was the combination of many different blocks of land that were squeezed together. This land, in turn, had formed other continents before it became part of Pangaea.

The continents known today started forming a little more than 250 million years ago. The land that formed Europe and Asia split off first and moved northeast. Over the next 50 million years, North America separated and moved northwest. These two continents formed the boundaries of the North Atlantic and the North Sea of Europe.

Scientists call the mass of land left behind Gondwana. The name comes from the work of a nineteenth-century geologist, Eduard Suess. He believed there once had been two supercontinents covering earth's southern hemisphere. According to Suess, they linked the lands of India, Africa, South America, Antarctica, and Australia. Suess did not believe the continents moved. He thought that the continents had been joined by land bridges that had sunk into the oceans. Suess gave the name Gondwanaland to the supercontinent that he thought contained India. Gond-

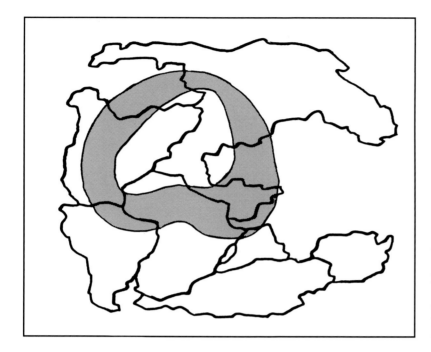

This map of Pangaea shows the position of the continents millions of years ago. The dotted line represents "the ring of oil," where most of the world's oil fields have been found.

wana was an old kingdom that once occupied part of India.

Gondwana started breaking up sometime between 100 million and 150 million years ago. Antarctica went south. Australia headed west. India started its long journey over the equator toward Asia. And Africa and South America separated, with the southern Atlantic Ocean forming in between them. Over the last 100 million years, the continents have been moving into their present positions.

Scientists have been able to track the movement of the continents by combining information from different fields. Geologists analyze rock formations with an eye toward finding how far they traveled. Geophysicists use computers to move the tectonic plates backward along their most likely courses. Biologists study fossils of land-based animals that have been found on different continents. By finding out how old these fossils are, they can estimate when these

continents may have been connected. Even oil explorers have contributed to developing a view of the past. In the 1970s, a study by the Rand Corporation showed most of the world's oil fields formed a "ring of oil" when they were plotted on a map of Pangaea.

The Secret of Suspect Terranes

One of the more exciting areas of plate tectonic study is the field of suspect terranes. *Terrane* is a geology term referring to an entire, three-dimensional block of the earth's crust. Geologists use this word to distinguish terranes from terrains, which are surface sections of the crust. A suspect terrane is a block of land that does not seem to fit in the area where it is found. It was likely scooped up by a continent millions of years after it formed.

Geologists first noticed the phenom-

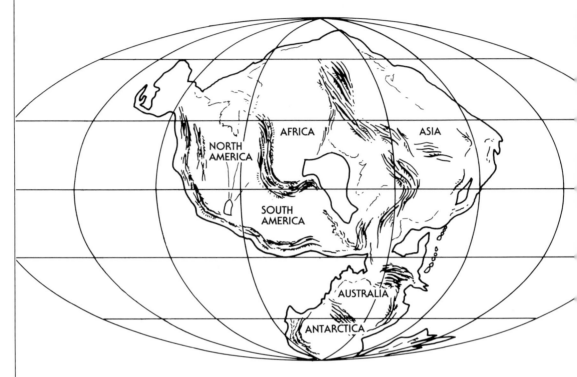

As continents and ocean floors continue to drift on their plates, the process of subduction appears to be gradually closing the Atlantic and Indian oceans. If this trend continues over the next 250 million years, the seven continents we know today will be reshaped into two supercontinents. North America, South America, Africa, Europe, and Asia will merge into one continent containing a huge inland sea—the only remnant of the Atlantic and Indian oceans. At the same time, Antarctica and Australia appear to be heading toward a merger to form the second supercontinent.

enon of suspect terranes during the 1970s. A team of geologists was studying fossils of microscopic animals in the Canadian province of British Columbia. They realized that the animal remains they were looking at had also been found elsewhere in the world. The remains were of creatures that had lived in what is now eastern Asia more than 250 million years ago. At that time, North America and eastern Asia were on oppo-

site sides of Pangaea. The only way the fossils could have appeared in British Columbia was if part of the land where they lived had been carried across the planet.

Terrane experts think the suspect terrane in British Columbia might have been transported on top of a long-lost tectonic plate. This plate would have existed long before the Pacific Plate began to form. Geologic surveys of Alaska

The theory of plate tectonics has allowed people to decipher many puzzling questions about how the earth was formed. The activity of hot magma creeping to the surface of the earth from underground and through volcanoes is just one of the many activities explained by the theory.

show most of the state is made up of similar terranes. Scientists think that some of the terranes are old volcanic islands that were plastered against the leading edge of North America. Other evidence has been found that supports this idea. Probably the most dramatic evidence is the deposits of seafloor lava and fossils found in the state of Idaho. Most of the land in the San Francisco Bay Area is also made up of these terranes.

Suspect terranes are forcing many geologists to rethink their theories about how landforms are created. They are helping other scientists identify long-lost continents that existed millions of years ago. And they are aiding still other scientists in the construction of possible future continents.

Scientists have been able to form a number of pictures of what earth will look like in the far future. They have done this using computers to project the paths tectonic plates will probably take. In a sense, the scientists are like drivers following a road map. They know how the plates moved in the past. They know how they are acting today. With this knowledge, they have been able to make an educated guess about how the plates will behave tomorrow.

A New Supercontinent in 250 Million Years

Right now, scientists think a new Pangaea will form in about 250 million years. This new supercontinent will combine North and South America, Africa, and most of Asia. Australia and Antarctica will form a smaller supercontinent to the south.

The new Pangaea will be centered around a huge inland sea. This sea will be all that is left of a former African Rift Ocean. Today, the African Rift is the beginning of a tectonic ridge jutting south from the Arabian Peninsula. It is responsible for the Great Rift Valley that is splitting the eastern coast of Africa from the rest of the continent. Scientists think the rift will form a young ocean 100 million years from now. This ocean will grow for about another 100 million years. Before long, however, it will be fenced in by South America and the former eastern African coast. This future African Rift Ocean then will be similar to the Mediterranean Sea.

The Future of Plate Tectonics

As fantastic as it sounds, this model of the future is really just a good scientific guess. For all the advances they have made, scientists still do not fully under-stand the process of plate tectonics. Fortunately, they know what questions they have to answer next.

The most important of these questions is "What makes the plates move?" This question is much like the one that Alfred Wegener could not answer when discussing continental drift. Modern scientists are closer to solving this mystery than Wegener was, however. They think the movement of the earth's mantle may be pulling the plates along their paths. And they think the heat of the earth may be providing the power to move the mantle.

Convection currents are loops of

Some scientists believe that hot magma rising to the surface may be the force that moves the plates. Here, lava rises up from beneath the earth like water in a pot.

warmth that form in heated liquid or gas. For example, water heating in a pot rises to the surface and spreads out over the cooler water. In turn, the cooler water sinks to the bottom of the pot. Then, it too heats up and rises. The action creates a cycle of hot water replacing cool water in a continual loop. The process repeats itself until all the water is at the same temperature.

Scientists think the same process is happening inside the earth. Hot magma from deep in the mantle may be rising like water in a pot. If so, it spreads under the crust and sinks back toward the center of the earth as it cools. Friction from this circulating magma may be the force moving the tectonic plates. If true, this theory—called the convection model—would explain many of the features of plate tectonics. The Mid-Ocean Ridge would mark areas where hot magma rises. Subduction trenches would show where cooling magma sinks.

It may be that we will never really know why the plates move. Scientists can only speculate about what is happening under the crust of the earth. Their ideas about convection in the mantle are based on secondhand evidence. This evidence comes from studies of sea-floor temperature, earth's magnetism, and other forces. They cannot make any direct observations about the mantle. Not only is it too hot, but it is too deep. The longest drills can go only a fraction of the way through the crust. There is no way to pierce through to the mantle.

We Know Better Now

Whatever discoveries the future brings, we now have a more accurate view of our world. Modern instruments and techniques have finally allowed scientists to discover how the world's surface behaves. But this knowledge would have been useless if some scientists had not been able to see past the well-accepted views of their time. It may be that future scientists will come to even more amazing conclusions than we can imagine today. Nonetheless, the understanding of plate tectonics has forever changed the way we see our planet.

Glossary

■ ■

anticline: A dome-shaped fold in the ground that often forms traps for oil deposits.

black smoker: An underwater vent of hot, mineral-rich water heated by contact with rising magma.

continental drift: An old theory of how the earth's surface formed, stating that the continents had floated or plowed through earth's crust to their present positions.

contraction: The cooling and shrinking of the earth's interior. It was once believed that this process caused the earth's surface to fold and collapse, forming mountain ranges and ocean basins.

convection: The circulation of heat in a liquid or a gas.

core sample: A column of rock or soil drilled out of the ground.

crust: The surface or outer rock layer of the earth, including the continents and the tectonic plates.

earthquake: A heavy shaking of the ground caused by movement along a fault or by volcanic activity.

epicenter: The point on the ground above the center of an earthquake.

erosion: The gradual wearing down of the land caused by wind, rain, and other forces.

explosion seismology: The study of shock waves in the ground caused by dynamite or other explosives.

Fathometer: A device that uses sound waves to measure the distance between a ship's bottom and the seafloor.

fault: A line or fracture in the earth where blocks of rock move past each other.

fault creep: The gradual movement of land along a fault.

focus: The general area underground where an earthquake is centered.

geologic basin: A large depression in the surface of the earth often formed in the early stages of a developing rift zone; can also be a lake bed or the floor of a young ocean.

geologic time: The immense amount of time it takes for the earth to move continents, build mountains, form oceans, and so on.

geology: The study of the earth's rocks and landforms.

geothermal energy: Energy created using steam and hot water pumped from geysers and hot springs.

Gondwana: A prehistoric supercontinent formed by the breakup of another supercontinent called Pangaea.

guyots: Flat-topped underwater mountains that once poked above the surface of the sea.

hot spots: Areas in the middle of

tectonic plates where superhot magma burns through the crust.

Kashima: In Japanese legend, the god who prevented earthquakes by restraining the movement of a giant catfish.

kerogen: An ooze formed by organic matter as it begins to decay and form oil.

land bridges: Huge spans of land once thought to have connected the continents.

Love waves: Seismic waves that shake the surface of the ground back and forth.

liquefaction: The process of shaking sediments until they are loose enough to act like a liquid.

magma chamber: An underground cavern created as magma rises toward the surface of the earth.

magnetometer: A machine that can detect and measure changes in magnetic fields.

magnitude: A measurement of an earthquake's power according to the Richter scale.

Mid-Atlantic Ridge: A segment of the Mid-Ocean Ridge that runs down the middle of the Atlantic Ocean.

Mid-Ocean Ridge: An underwater mountain chain formed along a forty-thousand-mile rift in the earth's surface. It is the source of earth's seafloor.

Namazu: In Japanese legend, a giant catfish that lived under the world and created earthquakes by wiggling its body.

nodules: Balls of minerals, mainly manganese, that form in the ocean.

ocean basin: The deep seafloor surrounded by continental shelves.

oil: A thick sludge formed by the controlled decomposition of organic matter. It is used to make fuel, fabric, plastic, and other materials.

Pangaea: Formed from the Greek words meaning "all" and "land," the name given to a supercontinent thought to have existed about 300 million years ago; also the name of a supercontinent scientists think will exist about 250 million years from now.

Pele: In Hawaiian legend, the goddess of fire.

plates: Huge slabs of rock that make up the surface of the earth.

plate tectonics: The creation, movement, and destruction of earth's surface plates; also the study of this process.

primary waves: The first seismic waves recorded in an earthquake; they move by compressing and pulling apart the rock they travel through.

Rayleigh wave: A slow-moving seismic wave that moves through the ground like an ocean wave.

Richter scale: A system of measuring the power of an earthquake by comparing the time between primary and secondary waves with the earthquake's strongest seismic waves.

rift zone: A crack in the earth's crust where magma pushes up to form a new seafloor.

Ring of Fire: The name given to the string of volcanoes that lie along the edge of the Pacific Ocean. These volcanoes are formed along or near tectonic plate subduction areas.

salt dome: A huge block of salt buried in soil or sedimentary rock that often forms traps for oil deposits.

seafloor spreading: The movement of the seafloor away from the earth's rift zones and toward its subduction zones.

secondary waves: The second seismic waves to be recorded in an earthquake. They shake the ground vertically and horizontally and cause most of the damage in an earthquake.

seismic gap: An area of a fault that has not been the scene of a recent earthquake.

seismic waves: Shock waves in the ground caused by earthquakes, volcanic eruptions, or the detonation of dynamite or other explosives.

seismograph: A machine that can record the passage of seismic waves.

seismology: The study of earthquakes.

seismometer: A machine that transmits impulses from passing seismic waves to a monitor or a recording device.

stratigraphic trap: An oil trap formed by the changing density or composition of underground rock layers.

structural trap: An oil trap formed by the shape of the ground.

suspect terrane: Blocks of land that seem to have been formed far from where they are found.

terrane: A three-dimensional block of the earth's crust.

transform fault: A fault formed near an underwater ridge by touching seafloor segments that move in opposite directions.

tsunami: A giant sea wave caused by an underwater earthquake or a huge volcanic eruption.

volcano: A mountain or island created by lava erupting from inside the earth.

volcanology: The study of volcanoes.

Vulcan: In Roman mythology, the god of fire and metalworking.

zebra striping: Patterns of weak and strong magnetic fields in the seafloor formed by magnetically charged particles that record past changes in earth's magnetic field.

For Further Reading

■ ■

Isaac Asimov, *How Did We Find Out About Earthquakes?* London: Essex, 1978.

Robert D. Ballard, *Exploring Our Living Planet.* Washington, DC: National Geographic Society, 1983.

John W. Harrington, *Dance of the Continents.* Los Angeles: Jeremy P. Tarcher, 1983.

Gregory Vogt, *Predicting Volcanic Eruptions.* New York: Franklin Watts, 1989.

Works Consulted

Bruce A. Boldt, *Earthquakes*. New York: W.H. Freeman, 1988.

Allen A. Boraiko, "Earthquake in Mexico," *National Geographic Magazine*, May 1986.

Jon Erickson, *Volcanoes and Earthquakes*. Blue Ridge Summit, PA: TAB Books, 1988.

Ann Finkbeiner, "California's Revenge," *Discover*, September 1990.

Rick Gore, "Our Restless Planet Earth," *National Geographic Magazine*, August 1985.

Allan G. Lindh, "Earthquake Prediction Comes of Age," *Technology Review*, February/March 1990.

Los Angeles Times, "Volcano Watch," October 1990.

Bart McDowell, "Eruption in Colombia," *National Geographic Magazine*, May 1986.

Russel Miller, *Continents in Collision*. Alexandria, VA: Time-Life Books, 1983.

Richard Nehring, *Giant Oil Fields and World Oil Resources*. Santa Monica, CA: Rand Corp., 1978.

Martin Schwarzbach, *Alfred Wegener, the Father of Continental Drift*. Madison, WI: Science Tech, 1986.

E.N. Tiratsoo, *Oilfield of the World*. Houston: Gulf Publishing, 1986.

Bryce Walker, *Earthquake*. Alexandria, VA: Time-Life Books, 1982.

Jonathan Weiner, *Planet Earth*. New York: Bantam Books, 1986.

Index

About the Author

Free-lance writer Sean M. Grady is the youngest writer for *The Encyclopedia of Discovery and Invention*. Originally a physics major, he received a Bachelor of Arts degree in print journalism from the University of Southern California in 1988. While in college, he worked for the entertainment section of the *Los Angeles Times* as a reporting intern; for *California Magazine* as a research intern; and for the City News Service of Los Angeles, a local news wire, as a general assignment reporter. In the two years after his graduation, Mr. Grady specialized in business reporting and worked as business editor of *The Olympian*, a daily newspaper in Olympia, Washington. Mr. Grady currently lives in Lacey, Washington.

Picture Credits

■ ■